**TS-138
Keeping
and
Breeding
Budgerigars**

***Title page:*** **Budgerigars are the favorite choice of many bird fanciers because of their small size, hardiness, and pretty appearance.**

**Photo credits:** Dr. Herbert R. Axelrod, H. Bielfeld, Michael Gilroy, Ray Hanson, Fred Harris, A. Jesse, Barbara Kotlar, Harry V. Lacey, Louise Van der Meid, Ron and Val Moat, Horst Müller, Aaron Norman, H. Reinhard, L. Robinson, Vince Serbin, Norma Veitch, Vogelpark Walsrode, and Wayne Wallace.

Originally published in German by Albrecht Philler Verlag under the title *Wellensittiche.*© Albrecht Philler Verlag GmbH, 4950 Minden, 1983.



*T.F.H. Publications, Inc. is the world's largest publisher of good books about pets of all kinds.*

Distributed in the UNITED STATES by T.F.H. Publications, Inc., One T.F.H. Plaza, Neptune City, NJ 07753; in CANADA to the Pet Trade by H & L Pet Supplies Inc., 27 Kingston Crescent, Kitchener, Ontario N2B 2T6; Rolf C. Hagen Ltd., 3225 Sartelon Street, Montreal 382 Quebec; in CANADA to the Book Trade by Macmillan of Canada (A Division of Canada Publishing Corporation), 164 Commander Boulevard, Agincourt, Ontario M1S 3C7; in ENGLAND by T.F.H. Publications Limited, Cliveden House/Priors Way/Bray, Maidenhead, Berkshire SL6 2HP, England; in AUSTRALIA AND THE SOUTH PACIFIC by T.F.H. (Australia) Pty. Ltd., Box 149, Brookvale 2100 N.S.W., Australia; in NEW ZEALAND by Ross Haines & Son, Ltd., 82 D Elizabeth Knox Place, Panmure, Auckland, New Zealand; in the PHILIPPINES by Bio-Research, 5 Lippay Street, San Lorenzo Village, Makati Rizal; in SOUTH AFRICA by Multipet Pty. Ltd., Box 235 New Germany, South Africa 3620. Published by T.F.H. Publications, Inc. Manufactured in the United States of America by T.F.H. Publications, Inc.

# BUDGERIGARS

MAJA MÜLLER-BIERL

**Budgerigars are ideal pets in homes that cannot accommodate other domesticated animals.**

# Contents



*The name "budgerigar" is derived from a word in the language of the Australian aborigines:* bedgerigah.

*Budgerigar: a small, beautifully colored member of the parrot family. Also referred to as a "budgie."*

# Preface

At some stage everyone is a beginner—every fancier every breeder. In the specialized literature he does not always find what he needs—namely a proper first introduction, advice, hints that often have become second nature to experienced breeders and consequently are no longer mentioned by them. The reader of this volume is not expected to have any previous knowledge of budgerigars nor of woodwork either. Becoming a good breeder does not necessarily imply being able to make one's own nest-boxes.

While early volumes on budgerigars in the main bore the stamp of years of experience on the part of their authors, this present volume seeks to provide an introduction on as broad a basis as possible. The literature on birds in general has become more extensive in recent years. Behavioral scientists have

**Budgerigars are beautiful birds that are interesting and easy to care for. You may find them so delightful that you'll wind up with several!**

**A color variety of budgerigar called lutino. Some budgerigar fanciers consider this bright yellow color to be one of the prettiest of all the budgie color varieties.**

also become interested in the budgerigar. Over and above that, important veterinary works have been published and the recommendations of experienced veterinarians particularly will be taken into account here. Some of the chapters in this book therefore may be of interest to more experienced breeders, too—as has been said, "... one never stops learning where bird-fancying is concerned."

The author would like to take this opportunity to express her special gratitude to Dr. J. Steinbacher for his friendly support and for his advice regarding societies and journals. My thanks, also, for advice and/or reference material to Dr. Lohr, Staatl. Tierärztl. Untersuchungsamt Aulendorf, Herr Schwarzberg (AZ), Herr Siepmann (DKB), Herr Bischofberger (Exotis), and the companies Vitakraft, Bremen, and Osram, Munich.

Maja Müller-Bierl
Salem 1983

*"... one never stops learning where bird-fancying is concerned."*

# Keeping and General Management

*"Biologically, breeding in colonies has many advantages . . ."*

## THE BUDGERIGAR IN AUSTRALIA

In their native homeland, Australia, budgerigars live in flocks, in association with many members of their own species. They breed in colonies, i.e., their territory is restricted to the nest. The individual pairs of these parakeets breed at very close range to one another. "The peculiar growth of the eucalyptus, which from a single rootstock forces up about eight to twelve trunks, white of bark and six meters (19.8 feet) tall, with scant-leafed tops and countless knot-holes, favors this business to a great degree. Every hollow stem, every knot-hole, even, if necessary, every suitable space inside the rootstock is used for nest-building," reports Engelhart. Biologically, breeding in colonies has many advantages, two of which are better protection from enemies, since many eyes can see more than just two, and mutual stimulation when it comes to breeding.

Birds of prey are dangerous enemies to the budgerigars. There is a report, for example, of two or three budgerigars having been taken by a hawk at a watering place. A budgerigar which has spotted a bird of prey immediately reacts by uttering loud warning cries, and the whole flock scatters in all directions. Afterwards their call-notes bring the birds back together again.

## FUNDAMENTAL ASPECTS OF AVIARY CONSTRUCTION

Being kept in an aviary together with members of its own species best meets the natural requirements of the budgerigar for a gregarious way of life and for breeding in a colony.

While the budgerigar has adapted to temperate climate and is able to stay outdoors at temperatures of down to −20°C (−4°F) provided it is always kept outdoors, it is advisable to add an indoor shelter to the aviary. The shelter should have a window through which natural light can enter. Elongated constructions, the outdoor enclosures of which all face in the same direction, have proved successful. Drafts must be avoided. The roof should be well insulated so that the inside of the aviary does not get too hot in the summer and too cool in the winter. The indoor compartments are often separated by solid walls to make sure the inmates disturb one another as little as possible. The walls should be smooth to facilitate easy cleaning. If wood is used for the construction (also for the framework of the outdoor aviary), it may need to be covered with wire netting of a narrow mesh because of the budgerigars' gnawing-urge (especially that of the females). It should also be given a smooth coat of non-toxic paint. There must be no gaps or cracks anywhere in the construction to allow insects or vermin to enter. Any parts made of iron must be painted with an anti-corrosion agent. The wire netting between the compartments must be of a mesh narrow enough to prevent the birds from poking their heads through it. It is best to use a double layer of wire for the partitions; then there is no problem if the keeper wants to stock the aviary with different birds (such as lovebirds, for example) at a later stage. The outside wire should also consist of a double

**Budgerigars can thrive and be perfectly content within the confines of an aviary.**

*Aviary: a spacious enclosed area used for housing birds.*

layer—the external one of an extra-narrow mesh to prevent mice from entering through the holes. Double wire netting ensures that birds of prey or cats cannot injure the parakeets when the latter hang suspended from the wire as they like to do, often sleeping in that position as well. Additional protection against cats can be provided in the form of an electric cattle fence which is installed around the aviary. The aviary needs a good foundation so that mice and rats cannot get in from below. Mice and rats do not merely destroy large quantities of food; they can also be a danger to young birds. Above all, however, they are potential vectors of disease.

"Experience has shown that the floor of the outdoor flight is the greatest source of danger with regard to infections," is the observation of well-known veterinarians who point out that, according to their calculations, ten budgerigars drop 36 g (1.26 ounces) of excreta per day which accumulate mostly on the floor of the outdoor aviary and, together with food left-overs, get worked into the earth by rain, earthworms, and micro-organisms if, as is frequently the case, the aviary floor consists of natural soil. The veterinarians maintain further, "The basic prerequisite for hygienic

***Opposite:* Due to the many mutations in color and pattern, the budgerigar is one of the most variegated and beautiful of birds.**

**A colony of budgerigars. Adequate flight space is very important for the healthy development of these birds.**

*"... a budgerigar fancier ... should be perfectly happy to devote the necessary time to cleaning."*

bird-keeping is a smooth concrete floor" which, ideally, should slope slightly to make it easy to clean. The concrete floor must be cleaned often. They experimented with flights above ground-level (for budgerigars, e.g.). This means that wire netting is put across at a height of about 80 cm (32 inches) so that the bird is no longer in contact with the soil. I personally reject this method of bird-keeping. While due to wire-floor keeping the fact that an 85% success rate could be achieved with the ruffed grouse (hitherto considered virtually impossible to raise) is indeed impressive, where budgerigars are concerned this need for a wire floor does not really exist. Running about on the ground is, after all, as much part of the budgerigar's natural behavior as flying and perching on the upper branches. I feel that a budgerigar fancier for whom breeding is a hobby should be perfectly happy to devote the necessary time to cleaning. It has been reported of

One method of holding a budgerigar. At first, your pet may resist your attempts to hold him, but if you are gentle and patient he can get used to the idea.

**Budgerigars are interesting and personable birds that can make wonderful companions.**

budgerigars observed in Australia, "As a rule they keep to the highest tops of these trees (eucalyptus), but for feeding they come down to the ground." For reasons of hygiene, I recommend a smooth concrete floor which is covered with a layer of clean sand. To meet the behavioral needs of this species, a bowl of soil with seedlings and bird-food plants can be put on the ground and replaced as necessary.

The height of the compartments of the aviary should be adapted to the aviculturist's body size to minimize the need for stooping when doing the cleaning. The flight-hole is best equipped with a flap or door which can be closed, to shut the birds out while cleaning is in progress. Partial roofing of the outdoor flight provides shady and dry spots. The construction of such an aviary requires a certain amount of manual skill, of course.

*"Shrubs planted close to the aviary must not be poisonous."*

It is now also possible to buy a range of ready-made aviaries. Breeders should give their budgerigars the opportunity to fly.

## CHOOSING THE LOCATION FOR AN AVIARY

Ideally, the aviary should be constructed or erected so that the outdoor compartments face south or southeast. The site should be sunny, airy but not drafty. The planting of hedges and shrubs can help to ensure this. Shrubs planted close to the aviary must not be poisonous. There must be no branches overhanging the aviary which could rub

**It is fine to provide your budgie with a natural perch as long as it comes from a tree that hasn't been chemically treated.**

against the latter in windy weather. It has been suggested that this can cause Australian parakeets to panic and incubating females to leave the nest-box forthwith. The explanation for this is assumed to be a flight reflex which has evolved in the parakeets in response to scratching noises such as those caused by the movements of monitor lizards which have endangered them for thousands of years by crawling up trees and clearing out their nesting hollows.

## AVIARY EQUIPMENT

The number of perches must be adapted to the number of occupants of the compartment. The perches should be fitted provisionally to start with. If the breeder notices that certain spots are preferred, he will ensure that sufficient perching facilities are available there. This is particularly important where roosting places are concerned. If one fails to adapt to the birds' needs, a lot of squabbling ensues. The birds then also hang on the wire netting more than

**Your pet shop has a variety of sturdy, well constructed cages from which you can choose. Be sure to select one with bars that run horizontally because budgies like to climb, and this is difficult to do with vertical bars.**

**Budgies are alert, curious little birds that are interested in the activities of their companions.**

they would otherwise. The perches should be of varying thicknesses. Natural twigs with bark (unsprayed) are the best option. They must be placed so that the lower ones are not soiled by droppings from birds sitting higher up. Most importantly, they must not be placed above seed dishes or water containers. A single feeding place is not sufficient. If too few seed dishes are provided, the immature birds are

*"... perches should be of varying thicknesses."*

**To keep a bird from flying free or to make it easier to tame, some hobbyists recommend clipping the bird's wing. The clipped wing feathers will grow back after the bird has molted.**

chased away from them by the adults and could die of starvation. Food and water must be located in dry, shady spots. To enable the birds to utilize all the available space, it is best to put the seed dishes on the floor. This is in keeping with the birds' natural habits, and it encourages not only horizontal flights but also vertical ones, thus doing something towards meeting their need for varied movement. I never put water troughs or water bowls directly on the floor, however, as these tend to

**What have we here? If you are going to let your pet out of his cage, be sure you are nearby to supervise his explorations.**

**A colony of budgies in a well-lit indoor aviary. An important factor in planning an aviary is making sure that the occupants will have the longest possible flight space.**

grow moldy underneath if this is done. The water level inside the containers must not be too high when the young fledge and are still clumsy, or they might drown in them. It is important too that a water container never stands in the immediate proximity of the feeding place; otherwise, the water might become contaminated and the food might get wet and grow moldy.

*"If breeding is intended during the cold season . . . a heated breeding room or indoor shelter is absolutely essential."*

**HEATING**

If breeding is intended during the cold season, too, a heated breeding room or indoor shelter is absolutely essential. The temperature should range from about 15°C (59°F)at night to 26°C (80°F) by day and must be checked up on. If the heating breaks down, the young are at risk, particularly those the adult birds have recently stopped brooding; under-heated birds no longer open their beaks for food and hence do not get fed. The risk is especially great in the case of a single nestling. Several nestlings huddled close together lose less warmth. Sudden drops in temperature in the spring are dangerous if the nest-boxes are not kept inside a heated room. Broods produced early in the year

**A lovely lutino budgie. Any natural perch that you offer your budgie should be non-poisonous and free from insecticides.**

Budgerigars are intelligent, playful birds. If you acquire a pair of them, they can be companions for each other and their antics will delight you.

are, therefore, always more at risk. This risk can be reduced by utilizing a nest-box heater (available on the market).

## LIGHTING

During the cold season when the days are shorter the day must be extended by means of artificial illumination if young are to be raised. Otherwise the adult birds do not have sufficient time to take in enough food. Switching off the light must not catch the birds unprepared, else

If you want to provide toys for your budgie, a visit to your local pet shop is a must. Your pet shop dealer offers a wide variety of play items for birds of all kinds.

*"In complete darkness budgerigars tend to grow frantic during the night; a noise can set them off."*

the females can not find their way into their nest-box. The consequences would be that the eggs would grow cold, newly-hatched chicks would get too cold. Ideally, the light should be switched on and off at the same time every day by means of a time-switch. At the same time the night-light (8 watts, for example) must switch itself on. In complete darkness budgerigars tend to grow frantic during the night; a noise can set them off. It is the budgerigars' natural instinct to react to danger by making a frantic getaway. In the wide open spaces of the Australian

A well-equipped aviary includes adequate provision for fresh clean water for the occupants. The water bottles shown here are ideal because the birds cannot soil their contents.

Wild budgerigars of the Australian plains feed on various grass seeds. Accordingly, an important part of your budgie's diet should be a mixture of various seeds.

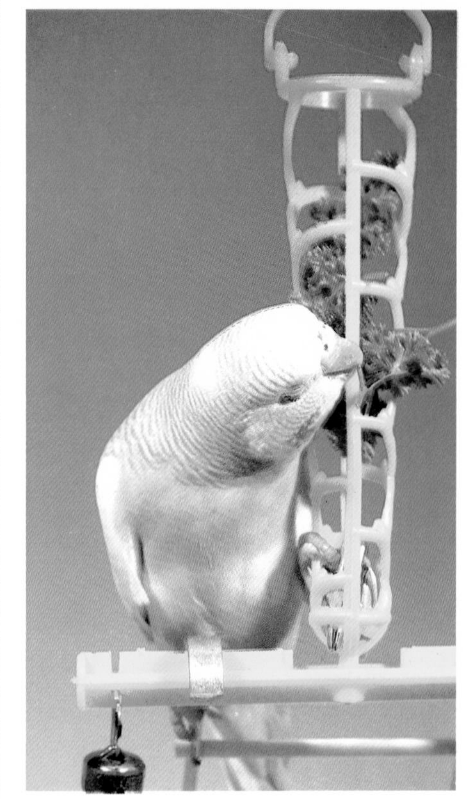

**Any green food that you offer your budgie should be clean and free of pesticides.**

**Budgerigars are social birds that can enjoy feeding together.**

steppe this makes sense, of course. But in the domesticated budgerigar this innate reflex-like behavior has been preserved and in a confined space it leads to aimless, frenzied flying about. The consequence of such wild behavior is that the birds calm down only with great difficulty, and serious injuries may result.

## NOISE NUISANCE

The aviculturist Radtke describes the chatter of a biggish flock of budgerigars in an aviary as a "constant alternation between a murmuring and gurgling twittering or loud whistling—and croaking sounds which somebody with bad nerves cannot always tolerate. The call-note of the budgerigar is fairly loud and penetrating; louder still is the warning-croak; both have an infectious effect on members of the same species."

A court verdict in 1978 attracted a great deal of attention. A woman in Germany was forbidden to continue with the keeping or breeding of budgerigars in the aviaries in her garden. A lady in the immediate neighborhood had been feeling disturbed by the 30 budgerigars and 8 large parakeets and had brought a nuisance claim for noise against her. This happened in a residential area which consisted predominantly of detached houses with gardens. The arguments are of interest. The plaintiff did not dispute what matters primarily is not so much its measurable volume as its existing nuisance value irrespective of volume. The nuisance factor in this

**A compacted seed stick, shown here, is favored by some budgies. Don't be surprised if your budgie develops a fondness for some kinds of seeds and ignores the rest.**

that the road traffic was causing a considerable amount of noise. But traffic noise, she argued, was something one had to put up with, not so the croaking and shrieking of exotic birds in large numbers. The court decided, "As regards noise of the kind in question, case is being increased considerably by the enforced 'anticipation of noise' even during quieter periods." The traffic noise did not affect the verdict one way or the other since it did not completely drown out the noise made by the birds. In this case there were other

*Birdseed: a blend of various types of seed that is used as a food for birds. It can include millet, niger, and linseed.*

A light green budgerigar.

A sky blue budgerigar.

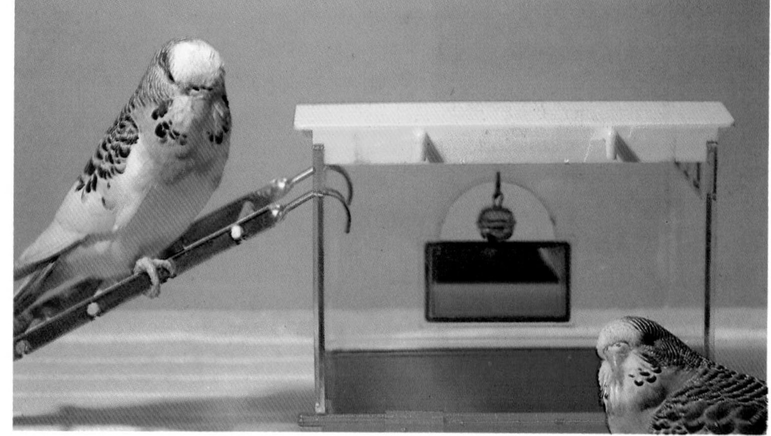

**Your budgie should have the opportunity for regular exercise.**

neighbors who did not regard the twittering of the 38 birds as a nuisance.

Birdsong often gets a mixed reception. Many a blackbird has been cursed for its song early in the morning. A veterinary anatomist from Berlin has been quoted as observing: "How beautifully quiet and peaceful it must have been in the Triassic, Jurassic and Cretaceous periods! The murmur of the ocean waves, the whispering of the wind in the ginkgo trees, and here and there the muffled gurgling of a dinosaur. But then came the birds with their syrinx (voice-box) at the fork of the windpipe and the resonance cavities of their air sacs; they thrust their beaks open and chirped, crowed, croaked, quacked, warbled, shouted, and howled—with the birds, noise came into the world!" The budgerigar fancier needs to be aware that some of his neighbors might derive no pleasure whatsoever from the twittering of his birds. It is important, therefore, to establish this *before* constructing an aviary. If the worst comes to the worst, the latter may have to resign himself to pursuing his budgerigar hobby inside closed rooms.

*Syrinx: the voice-box of a bird. This organ enables a bird to vocalize.*

**A bird swing, shown here, will afford your pet the chance to exercise his toes.**

## STACKED BREEDING UNITS

Most aviculturists who breed budgerigars for color and exhibiting prefer, at least while breeding is going on, to keep their birds in individual cages, each accommodating one pair, rather than in community

**A budgie will preen another budgie as scrupulously as he preens himself.**

*Aviculturist: One who pursues the hobby of raising or keeping birds.*

**In order to have healthy, happy budgerigars, you must provide them with an interesting and nutritious diet.**

*Breeding room: a room that is designated and specially equipped for breeding birds.*

aviaries. Such "batteries" can be started with one or two boxes (made by the hobbyist himself or purchased) and expanded as desired. The breeding room should not be used for human habitation. Suitable would be a basement room, for instance, in a house on a hillside, preferably with a large window facing south. Many aviculturists house their breeding birds in an outdoor aviary during the resting period—likewise the juvenile birds (which should be kept in a separate enclosure, if possible).

A home-constructed battery requires a certain amount of manual skill. All-plastic boxes are manufactured without joints and can be stacked on top of each other. The wire fronts are replaceable. When the drawer is pulled out a locking pendulum prevents the inmates from flying off. There are several lighting possibilities. Cleaning is very easy.

Not everyone can start off on a grand scale. It is possible to build a cage for which little if any manual skill is needed. A nest-box can be attached to this after the wire has been cut out. I have designed several metal cages and their construction, including the technique of fitting the wire. In addition, pet shops stock different types of nest-boxes at

**If you are going to keep but a single budgie, you should spend time with him on a regular basis. He will enjoy the attention.**

**The large white object in this budgie's cage is a cuttle bone, a source of minerals for many bird species.**

*Juvenile bird: a young bird that has yet to reach sexual maturity.*

**Many fanciers prefer to cover their pet's cage at night so that he is less likely to become upset by any disturbances near his cage.**

A cage with a sliding tray is convenient when it comes time to clean your budgie's cage.

A male budgerigar in a state of watchful attentiveness.

reasonable prices.

One important point is *lighting*. Natural daylight is always to be preferred to artificial light. However, the aviculturist who breeds his birds in a closed room, especially in the winter, will not be able to manage without a daylight substitute. Daylight tubes (with UV-components) should be fitted at a greater distance from the birds. As yet too little is known about the possible effects of direct irradiation. Where some varieties are concerned the spectral radiation distribution is very similar to daylight. These lamps are available in several forms—as tubes, for

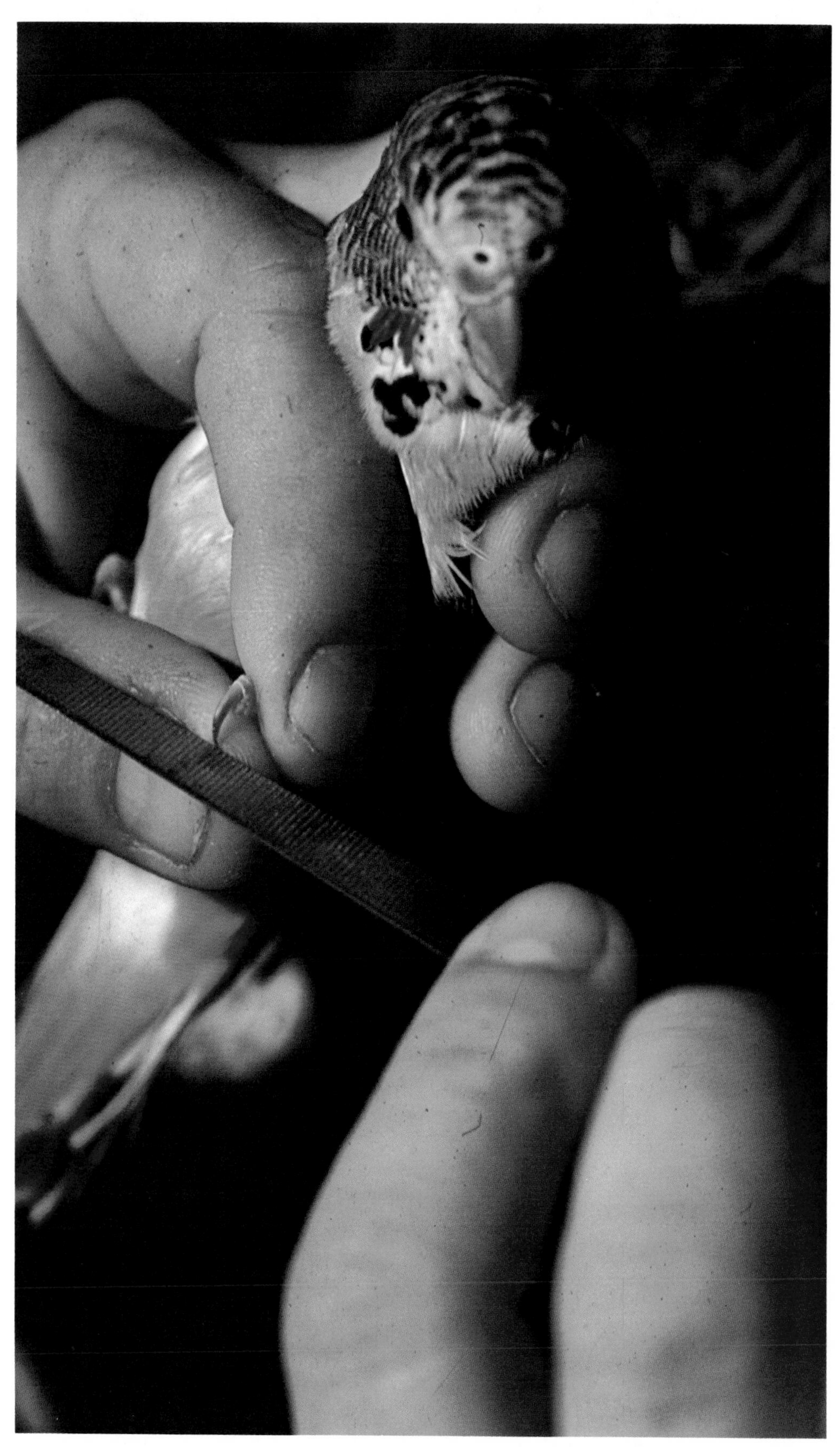

An ordinary nail file can be used to smooth ragged or too pointed claws. Be sure to file in one direction.

example, or in mushroom form with reflectors (250 watts, for instance). Because they give a lot of light and have a long lifespan, they are very economical. These lamps are best fitted at some distance from the birds (the instructions enclosed with the lamps should be carefully adhered to). It is advisable to provide an irregular, broken cover at the same time by way of imitating shade-throwing plants. In their natural environment the birds would not constantly expose themselves to sunshine without seeking some protection.

*"In their natural environment the birds [budgies] would not constantly expose themselves to sunshine without seeking some protection."*

**A budgie is never too busy playing to stop and enjoy the attention of a companion.**

With good looks and even temperaments, budgerigars have won many hearts in the bird fancy.

# Feeding

*Germinated food: grains (such as oats, wheat, and millet) that have sprouted. Germinated foods provide vitamins and are easy to digest.*

**Your budgie's food dish should be sturdy and easy to clean. A variety of eating utensils for your bird is available at your pet shop.**

**THE BUDGERIGAR IN AUSTRALIA**
Australia is very dry. Rainy seasons occur irregularly in many regions. Where there has been adequate rain and the steppe is beginning to grow green, large flocks of budgerigars suddenly appear. They feed mainly on seeds, for example those of the millet *Panicum*, which just happen to be half-ripe at the time the young are being raised; but insects have also been found among the contents of examined crops.

**HALF-RIPENED SEEDS AND GERMINATED FOOD**
We, too, can treat our budgerigars to seeds which are readily digestible and full of vitamins: the panicles of the various grasses, wheat and oats, provided they are free of chemical sprays. Otherwise we have germinated food at our disposal, which is a good substitute for the half-ripened seeds. Particularly suitable for the budgerigar are: oats (groats are no longer able to germinate), wheat, and millet (notably spray millet). If the grains are left to germinate, the vitamin content increases. Over and above that, due to the swelling alone, they become easy to digest. The birds like them best when

Given a proper diet, your budgerigar can be alert, active, and in good physical condition.

A yellow-faced gray budgie cock.

they have just begun to sprout and this is, in fact, when they are at their most valuable. In order to germinate, they need room temperature. It is important, particularly during the warmer months of the year, to rinse the grains in a sieve under a sharp jet of water. Depending on what temperatures prevail, leave the grains to stand covered with water in a shallow container, no deeper than 3 cm (1.2 inches) for 12 to 24 hours. Then drain them well and let them stand for an additional 12–24 hours. Immediately before use, rinse thoroughly once more. If, in spite of all precautions, the germinated grains smell

*"Mice are dangerous potential vectors of disease."*

musty or sour, do not on any account feed them to the birds. A well-respected veterinarian warns, "From the hygienic point of view it is important to note that droppings, for example." Mice are dangerous potential vectors of disease. For the birds, the greatest danger is represented by *Salmonella* and, in my experience,

**If you plan to keep budgies on a large scale, it is more economical to buy seed in large quantities. Be sure that the seed containers are tightly covered to keep moisture out.**

numerous disease-producing organisms can multiply in a damp, warm environment. Only a food which contains relatively few bacteria and fungi can, therefore, be used as starting material. It must be free of mouse pseudo-tuberculosis. The danger exists wherever mice have access to the food, which may already have happened before it was purchased. The bird-keeper would do well to keep his eyes open when buying seeds.

**A white budgie cock. Note the even quality of this bird's plumage.**

## BUYING AND STORING SEEDS

Correct storage of the seeds is essential if an infection with molds or mites is to be avoided. Seeds infected with mites lead to digestive disturbances. Moldy food is even more dangerous because of its poisonous effect. It has been strongly recommended that the moisture content of the grain must not exceed 15%. The relative atmospheric humidity must be kept below 70% and the temperature at around 10°C (50°F). Anyone who does not possess proper storage facilities should never buy seeds in bulk. One should be able to expect that the seeds are always fresh at the time of purchase.

*Mold: a fungal growth that can cause the decay of organic material.*

**Composition of food.** Where only a small number of birds are involved it is not worth one's while to mix the seeds oneself. In that situation it is better to rely on the budgerigar mixes marketed by experienced companies. These mixes should contain plenty of canary seed. A mix in the

**A wild budgerigar photographed in Australia.**

*Millet: a variety of grass cultivated in Europe and Asia. Its grain is utilized as a food source by man, and its seed is a common dietary component for many types of birds.*

following proportions is recommended: 60% millet, 30% canary seed, and 10% of a mix consisting of niger, linseed, oats, and some hemp. Very healthy for budgerigars, especially during the raising-period, are spray millet and the soft Japanese millet. I provide a specific commercial raising-food all the year 'round; outside the raising period it is in any case consumed in much smaller quantities.

Food plants for birds (chickweed, groundsel, dandelion, plantain, shepherd's purse, half-ripened grass-seeds, e.g.) are healthy, provided they have not been sprayed or exposed to excessive exhaust fumes. The same applies to fresh twigs. Where the latter are concerned make sure they are not covered with droppings from wild birds. [Caution: The birds' rings can get caught on thin twigs. The injuries sustained in this way will heal, as a rule, where the

The care and attention that you devote to your budgie will be reflected in his overall general appearance.

**Normal light green budgerigar.**

**Do not overdo it when offering green food as a part of your budgie's diet. Too much can cause stomach upset.**

keeper checks up on his birds at frequent intervals. There is a variety of unguents that can be used to treat swelling and scratches.]

That bird sand and lime (cuttle bone, grit) form part of the basic equipment goes without saying.

It is of prime importance that the food be clean. The seed dishes must be washed at regular intervals. Full seed dishes do not guarantee that adequate food is available. The keeper should take a closer look to make sure the seed dishes are not filled with just husks. The drinking water must be changed at least once a day and the water bowl washed. To boost the supply of minerals I add vinegar made from fruit to the drinking water (30/1). Synthetic vitamins should be administered where the diet contains insufficient vitamins, for instance when no raising-food is taken and green food is not available. Germinated food should be given only to stimulate the sexual instinct and during the raising period.

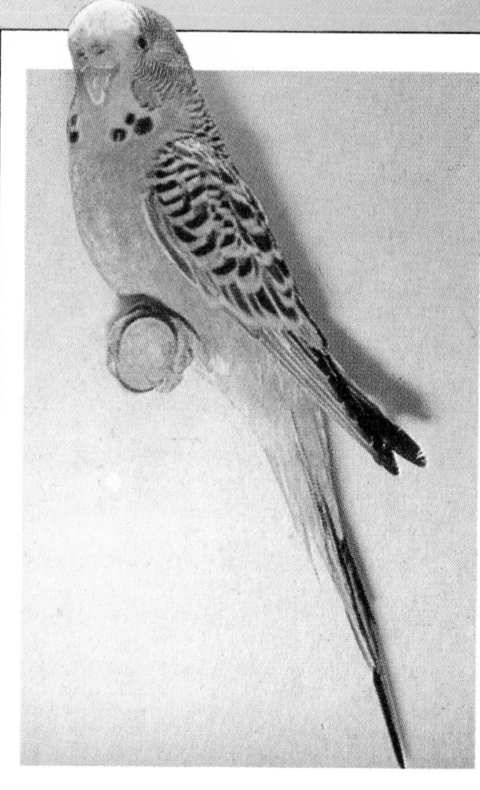

**A reflective object will capture a budgerigar's attention and entertain him for hours.**

*Grit: rough granular material that is part of a budgie's diet. Grit can be derived from a number of hard materials, such as oyster shell.*

If you are breeding your budgies strictly for hobby and are not seeking to produce a particular color variety, then the color of the birds selected for mating will not matter.

*Budgerigars have proved themselves to be interesting and amusing companions.*

# Breeding

An inquisitive opaline cobalt budgie cock peeping out from the nestbox.

Budgerigars are very eager to reproduce themselves, but keep in mind that these gregarious birds, which in their natural habitat breed in colonies, generally need stimulation from members of their own species. The budgerigar keeper who wants to try to breed his birds would, therefore, do better if he started off with at least two pairs.

There is a great temptation to acquire adult animals one might be able to use for breeding straightaway. Sometimes it does indeed happen that good breeding pairs are offered for sale (as for instance when a breeding battery is being dissolved). The new owner has no guarantee, however, that the birds will breed equally successfully on his own premises. It could happen that the changed keeping conditions have an adverse effect. Sometimes, too, a successful breeding pair is passed on at an advanced age when it is past its best. A clear warning to bear in mind: "Pairs offered for sale that are supposed to have a good breeding record often have something wrong with them. It has happened that an adult male and a juvenile male together were sold as a 'good breeding pair'. In other cases the male fails to fertilize, the female lays

**A successful budgie breeding program requires a commitment of time and effort on your part. Be sure you are fully aware of the responsibility associated with budgie breeding before you begin.**

*"The budgerigar keeper who wants to try to breed his birds would . . . do better if he started off with at least two pairs."*

**A nest box should be cleaned and disinfected before it is used.**

*Cere: a soft mass of tissue containing the nostrils. It is located at the base of the upper mandible in some birds, such as parrots.*

no eggs, lets them fall from the nest, devours them, does not incubate, deserts the newly-hatched chicks, eats their feathers, injures the young birds, throws them out of the nest, does not feed them, etc. There are many reasons for selling two attractive-looking animals. Unfortunately these can seldom be called genuine ones. Hobbyists who are new to bird-keeping invest all their hopes—and sometimes all their capital as well—in a 'good breeding-pair' like this and then find themselves deceived and bitterly disappointed. It is better, therefore, to buy juvenile animals."

Buying young animals has the advantage that the latter readily become acclimatized and are easily adapted to whatever type of food one would like to give them. The disadvantage, of course, is that mistakes can be made when it comes to sexing. In young budgerigars the cere does not yet show the characteristic color (blue in adult males, brown in adult females). It still looks pinkish in both sexes, although in some young females it can actually look more blue than pink. The only visible indicator of the female sex where young birds are concerned is a thin whitish ring around each nostril. It has been recommended taking the budgerigar in one's hand and tilting it head downward a few times. The greater vascularity of the head in the male then leads to violet blood-vessels becoming discernible in the cere. Mistakes can still be made, however, and it is not impossible that of the four budgerigars bought, three belong to the same sex. The reader who does not want to risk this would do better to make his purchase in the fall and try to get birds of the

**One reason for the budgerigar's popularity is its ability to breed in captivity.**

*"Before buying the birds one has selected it is important to check whether they are healthy. . . ."*

current year which already show the full adult colors. All he needs to do is to check up on the bird's ring. If it bears the impress of the current year, the bird is certain to be less than a year old and it is unlikely that breeding attempts have already been made with it.

Before buying the birds one has selected it is important to check whether they are healthy, at first from a greater distance. For, if one gets too close to them, even birds which do not feel well and otherwise sit about with ruffled feathers will anxiously smooth their plumage. A healthy bird does not present drooping wings; its eyes are clear. Above all it can fly. Pick up the bird and examine it carefully. The area around the nose and beak must be clean. Don't overlook the feet and legs. Check to see that the bird can stand properly, and that the toes can grip, and that all the claws are present. It is advisable to feel the pectoral musculature. If the keel of the breastbone projects sharply, the bird is emaciated. If the vent feathers are smeary or matted, the bird is suffering from diarrhea, which can have a variety of causes. Nest-young budgerigars still fly clumsily, sleep a lot during the day and at first are often seen to perch on

**Budgies are gregarious birds, occupied most of the time with one another. A single bird that is kept isolated for too long a time and not given any attention will not thrive and may even die.**

**Before embarking on breeding budgerigars, the breeder-to-be should give serious consideration as to what he will do with the newly raised birds.**

both legs, with the head tucked into the plumage, none of which is any cause for concern. Older birds sleep on one leg.

### THE CORRECT AGE FOR BREEDING

The budgerigar attains sexual maturity at three to four months. It can, therefore, help to preserve the species at a very early age. Where the Australian wild bird is concerned this is important since masses of budgerigars get killed by the severe droughts and heat waves. In 1931, for example, a farmer in Central Australia fished five tons of dead budgerigars out of a single watering-place for cattle. Another farmer removed 60,000 budgerigars from the watering-place for his

*Sexual maturity: the age at which a bird is able to breed and reproduce.*

Head study of a light green budgerigar.

A cobalt budgerigar. This is one of many lovely budgie colors available to fanciers. Note the size of the dots on the throat.

livestock. During relatively damp years, on the other hand, the budgerigars multiply on a massive scale, thus compensating for the losses.

**A trained budgie that is acclimated to his surroundings will not panic but perch quietly anywhere.**

*Molt: the shedding of an animal's external covering, such as feathers, skin, or horns, which is then replaced by new growth.*

For birds from spring and summer broods minimum age of ten months should be reached before they are used for breeding; for those from fall and winter broods, a higher age. The young of the first group pass through the molt relatively quickly; after about four months they show the adult colors. In late broods the molt from juvenile to adult plumage can take twice as long. If one waits, as usually recommended in the literature, until they are ten to twelve months old or more, they will no longer be in top breeding condition and good breeding results are doubtful. Whatever the birds' exact age, it is always an advantage when purchasing to get a male which is slightly older than the female. Not all of the wild budgerigar's behavior is innate. Some of it has to be learned (association with members of the same species, the search for food, etc.). Hence it can only be of advantage, as regards the preservation of the species, if a very young female chooses an

**Be sure that the birds you select for breeding are in top physical condition.**

experienced male. In captivity females do, in fact, prefer older males to younger ones if one gives them the choice. I, personally, was able to witness how my budgerigar hen rejected the male of its own age that had been bought at the same time and was bent on having a male from an adjacent cage which was two years older.

The maximum age of breeding animals which reproduce themselves at regular intervals is seven to nine years, at an average reproductive period of six years.

*Reproductive period: the length of time during an animal's life that it is able to reproduce.*

**COLONY BREEDING**

For colony breeding in the aviary the aviculturist

*"...[when colony breeding budgies] the pairs should come together of their own accord."*

needs at least a second compartment for those birds which are not in breeding condition, for juvenile birds that have not yet been sold, and for "retired" breeding animals. According to one authority, space of one cubic meter (35 cubic feet) per pair is essential as the birds are said to breed better in a less crowded breeding compartment. That the birds must match goes without saying, and not just as far as numbers are concerned; the pairs should come together of their own accord. No nest-boxes should be put up until this situation has resolved itself. If, in the end, there are still two females and two males which are unable to reach an agreement—perhaps because both females are determined to have the same male—it is better to take at least two of them out of the compartment. Partnerless males could disrupt mating. Supernumerary females develop dangerously aggressive tendencies. This can go so far as to lead to the death of incubating hens and the

**A handsome budgerigar family. The two birds in the center are the youngsters.**

When planning which birds to mate, be sure to take such factors as genetic traits and general behavior into consideration.

A breeding cage should be large enough to comfortably house both occupants. Ample perching space is also necessary.

*"Nowadays, breeding in the individual cage is generally preferred to colony breeding."*

destruction of the eggs. The cocks unfortunately do not defend their hens against other females. In the male budgerigar, actively defensive behavior is directed solely against male rivals. Generally speaking, the cock budgerigar is prepared to court every hen. Exceptionally it can happen that two hens peaceably share one nest-box and one male. This type of marriage stands a good chance where the breeding hole is big enough and the two females concerned are mother and daughter. There is a report of a case like this and what is interesting is that the shared cock was not the one the mother had had as a partner in the previous year.

A minimum of one and a half nest-boxes per pair is considered adequate, although two would be better. For the colony system I use identical nest-boxes throughout. Squabbles can still ensue, however, if two females are absolutely determined to have the same nest-box. In such cases it is best to hang up the box of contention in a different place. The dispute may repeat itself, however. Once one has been able to establish, by means of observation, why there is a preference for certain spots (light incidence, a particular height, e.g.) the problem can be resolved either by providing several more or less identical nesting facilities of the favored kind or, where this is not possible for reasons of space, by removing them altogether.

The following birds can be kept in association with budgerigars: cockatiels and plum-headed parakeets, zebra finches, and Java sparrows.

**BREEDING IN THE CAGE**

Nowadays, breeding in the individual cage is generally preferred to colony breeding. If the cages are standing very

Their beautiful coloration is one of the reasons why budgies are as popular as they are.

**Never let your budgie fly unrestrained outdoors as he may fly away from you and be lost forever.**

*Cage breeding: housing a breeding pair by themselves in a cage that has been equipped with a nest-box.*

close together—there is no reason why the adjacent pairs should not be able to see each other—the birds stimulate each other just as much as they do in the colony system. Now the aviculturist is able to match the pairs entirely in accordance with his wishes. This is what happens in the ideal case. However, the budgerigars' ideas as to the partners they want often differ greatly from that of the breeder's. Even in individual boxes it can happen, apparently, that two adjacent pairs are determined to mate with each other's partners. I never use force when it comes to matching. If a bird insists on having a sibling animal for a partner, I simply do not use it for breeding on that occasion. In some cases I may decide to exclude it from breeding altogether.

## ADVANTAGES AND DISADVANTAGES OF CAGE AND COLONY BREEDING

The main advantage of cage breeding is that the pairs can be put into their respective cages when they are in breeding condition and "in the mood" and that feeding can be adapted to the needs of each pair. Furthermore, the keeper can be certain that the entries in the book of descent are correct. This is one of the most serious drawbacks of colony breeding. The aviculturist can never actually be sure that the young raised by two adult birds are in fact genetically related to them. On the one hand, it can happen that inexperienced females lay their eggs into the wrong nest. On the other, some males have a tendency to mount other females while their own hen is busy incubating.

A further disadvantage of the colony system is that the breeding condition rarely reaches its peak in all the pairs at exactly the same time. This is largely compensated for by the strong stimulation effected by a breeding colony which, in my experience, ensures that all the pairs—provided they are healthy—raise their first brood of the season at approximately

When introducing a pair for breeding purposes, give them a few days to adjust to each other before offering the nest-box.

*Natural habitat: the environment in which a particular animal is most commonly found.*

the same time. During the second, subsequent brood there can be considerable differences in the timing, however, which may mean that when the first budgerigar family must be removed (so that there is no third brood) another pair is disturbed during a particularly sensitive period. A further disadvantage should be mentioned here: the individual animals receive a stimulus from the general breeding activity in the colony even when their own condition is less good, which is something that may not necessarily be obvious. The consequence of this can be that, although a hen lays eggs and incubates them, she does not feed at all or at least not for long. It may be assumed that in the birds' natural habitat in Australia not all the young budgerigars are raised successfully either. There, the breeding activity is triggered by external factors, namely rainfalls, regardless of the condition of each individual animal. Nonetheless it would be wrong to draw a parallel: what happens in Australia

**When introducing one budgerigar to another, it is important to note how they react to each other. If either bird harms the other or acts overly aggressive, the pair should be separated.**

is governed by natural selection. The survivors are undoubtedly more robust than our domesticated budgerigars.

Despite all the disadvantages of colony breeding mentioned, I still prefer it to cage breeding, not the least because it is more in keeping with the budgerigar's natural habits. The colony system is more time consuming, however. The aviculturist needs to have plenty of time for observation and check-ups. A great worry, with regard to colony breeding, are the female budgerigars that "run amok"—go from one box to another, attack incubating hens, destroy the eggs, and peck the chicks to death. Only observation can unmask them and eventually make it possible to remove them from the aviary. I once owned a female like that. In a mixed aviary with several cockatiels it had moved into a budgerigar nest-box with its partner. I noticed that the budgerigar hen often gazed into the cockatiel nest-boxes. One day I surprised her inside one of those upright boxes, down at the bottom; she was just damaging the first egg from the cockatiels' clutch. I immediately transferred her to a cage with her partner and the nest-box she had chosen, but she never laid an egg.

One advantage of colony breeding is that the young can be left inside the aviary until the second brood has fledged, provided the aviary is spacious. This affords an opportunity for charming observations which are not possible where cage breeding is concerned. There, the young have to be removed at an early stage. Because of the confined space, the adult birds soon behave aggressively towards the young.

Colony breeding enables the aviculturist to make many interesting observations, even if not all of them may be pleasant ones. Cage breeding, if carried out correctly, often gives more reliable and more

**A gray-green female budgerigar.**

*Brood: having or producing young; collectively, a group of young offspring of a particular animal, especially a bird.*

The conscientious budgie owner is always attuned to the overall physical appearance of his pet and thus to any changes that he may notice. Bright, clear eyes and full, smooth plumage are two signs of good health.

Due to successful selective inbreeding, many color varieties of budgies breed true to a predictable result. This very rare color variety is a recessive pied yellow-wing light green.

*"Cage breeding can teach the aviculturist a great deal about genetics and breeding for color."*

abundant breeding results with the added advantage of certainty as regards descent. Cage breeding can teach the aviculturist a great deal about genetics and breeding for color. Colony breeding tells him more about the nature, the behavior of these birds.

## FINAL MEASURES BEFORE THE BREEDING SEASON BEGINS

Before the nest-boxes are hung up everything should be cleaned thoroughly once more. For, while the females are sitting on the eggs, the birds should be disturbed as little as possible. It is advisable to check whether the perches are firmly fixed; any necessary minor repair work must be carried out now.

The nest-boxes must be hung up in such a way that they cannot drop and check-ups are possible at any time. This is particularly easy where the commercial breeding-boxes are concerned. In the aviary there are several possibilities of fixing the nest-boxes where they are safe from wind and water. If they are hung up on a nail (or fixed with wire, or put on a shelf

**Ringing, also known as banding, assists the budgie breeder in keeping records on his birds. The procedure should be performed when a chick is from five to eleven days old.**

**If you purchase a pair of budgies for breeding purposes, it is important that you first give them time to get acclimated to their new environment.**

provided for the purpose) at breast height or below, one only needs to open the lid if one wants to check up. The check-ups are especially easy from the food (or control) passage if the nest-boxes are hung up from the outside. It goes without saying that all the nest-boxes must be newly cleaned, disinfected, and intact. The bottom of the box should be covered with sterile litter (coarse sawdust being particularly advantageous) which will, however, be removed by many of the hens. The nest-boxes must not be provided until both partners are in breeding condition (smooth cere, complete plumage, liveliness).

**The younger a budgie is, the easier it is to hand-tame him.**

*Courtship: the process whereby a bird actively and persistently seeks the attention of a bird of the opposite sex.*

**It is the male budgerigar who usually initiates courtship.**

# The Breeding Cycle

## COURTSHIP

The breeding cycle begins with courtship. The initial advances are generally made by the male.

Twittering, he trips up and down the perch in front of the female, nods with the head, bows, knocks against the perch, the metal bars, the hen's beak with his beak, making gurgling noises, his pupils contracting in the excitement. The latter sign is soon caught by the female. Now her pupils grow narrow, too. She, too, trips up and down on the perch and nods with the head. The male's mating mood grows more aggressive; he kicks the hen with his foot. If the female flies off, the male follows her immediately in order to continue with his courtship behavior. It can also happen, however, that, stimulated by the proximity of other courting males, the hen takes on the active role, dances to and fro on the perch, nodding her head, and kicks the male in the

A single pair, if not given a nest box, does not usually breed, but they will stick close together.

flank with her foot. I have watched one of my hens do this repeatedly. Another aviculturist reports that he observed how a female, when mating was in full swing in the adjacent cage, adopted the copulatory position although her own male was not yet in the mood for mating.

The first intense courtship between the sexes does not necessarily result in mounting. It can end with the female crouching and begging the male for food, with the latter either obliging or in an aggravated manner attacking imaginary rivals, flying into the wire, courting metal bars and a variety of other objects, wildly flying around in circles, and eventually getting it out of his system. The more intense the courtship the less inclined is the cock to be distracted. When the female is ready the male mounts her.

*"The more intense the courtship the less inclined is the cock to be distracted."*

## THE ACT OF COPULATION

The female crouches on the perch with slightly raised wings and a hollowed back. The male mounts her, using his claws to gain a foothold or, sometimes, hanging on to her with the beak. Often the female turns her head

*Clutch: the total number of eggs produced by a hen at one time.*

back and the birds' beaks get hooked into each other. While sliding down the hen's back to press his cloaca against hers the male puts one extended wing around one of the female's flanks, which helps him to keep his balance. Inexperienced males, of course, do not always manage this at the first attempt. Once the cock is securely in position on top of the hen he changes over from one side to the other at shorter or longer intervals. The act of copulation can take several minutes.

### THE CLUTCH

Both the nesting hollow and the male's courtship behavior provide the stimulus for the female to lay eggs. Thus a clutch may be produced if the well-meaning keeper of a single budgerigar hen puts a nest-box into her cage to give her "a little house." But the mere presence of males, even when no nest-box has been provided, can trigger the laying of eggs. This also applies to tame hens kept on their own who regard their keeper as a partner substitute.

As soon as the hen gnaws at the nest-box, especially the entrance-hole, she shows both that she is in the mood for breeding and that she is interested in this particular nesting facility. Before long she inspects the box from the inside. The male also likes to slip inside the box. Often the two of them sit inside it for a longer period and one can hear soft twittering. If they do this for many weeks, however, without a single egg being laid, then there is something wrong. Females which are laying for the first time and which are more than a year old can be expected to produce the first egg eight days after copulation at the earliest and four weeks after it at the latest. Infertile females, unfortunately, are no rarity. Infertile males also occur. If pairs that get on well together produce unfertilized eggs, however, badly fitted or unsuitable perches are often to blame. Certain *types* of birds can have a problem: in coarsely feathered strong show specimens the feathers around the vent

**Two budgies kept together will bond to each other rather than to their owner, but they will keep each other occupied.**

**The body color of the wild budgerigar imported from Australia is light green with a yellow mask and black and yellowish markings on the wings. Today, budgies come in a wide spectrum of colors.**

A wide variety of toys that will occupy and amuse your budgie are available at your local pet shop.

*Incubation: the process whereby a hen warms eggs with her body heat and thus causes development of the embryos and the eventual hatching of the eggs.*

need to be trimmed prior to breeding.

The clutch usually consists of four to six eggs, although there may be as many as ten. They are pure white. The hen lays one egg every other day. The eggs are not identical in size. The eggs of show budgerigars are larger, on an average, than those of normal budgerigars. Smaller still were two eggs produced by budgerigars which were three months old. The weight of eggs belonging to normal birds was found to lie between about 1.3 and 2.9 g (.5–1 ounce).

## INCUBATION

The incubating is done solely by the hens. Some males are tolerated inside the box from time to time. It has been reported that there are, however, some males that help with the incubating. There was one male, for instance, which sat inside the box with the female during the whole of the incubation period. Sometimes the female looked out of the entrance-hole while the male remained perfectly still inside the box. The male only left the box to pick up food. The male feeds its female from the crop during the incubation period. The females seldom leave the box during the day, usually only to get rid of the feces which accumulate in large quantities throughout the incubation period (or from about two days before the first egg is laid). During

**Budgies are intelligent birds that make wonderful pets if they are tamed and treated properly.**

*"Even a day before hatching the peeping of the chick inside the egg can be heard."*

cage breeding it was observed how the female, with the male in tow, always climbed along the cage-wire at the other end of the cage, i.e., opposite to where the nest-box was, and there deposited its feces in a great pat. By means of a spatula the latter can be removed quite easily every day, which ensures that the cage remains relatively clean. Once the incubation period is over the frequency of defecation and the quantity deposited soon get back to normal.

Check-ups on the nest make sense in that they enable the breeder to remove damaged eggs. Above all, he must establish whether the female emerges from the box occasionally. It can happen that a hen dies while sitting on the eggs.

## HATCHING OF THE CHICKS

The first of the young hatches after an incubation period of about 18 days. The rest follow at intervals of roughly two days. Even a day before hatching the peeping of the chick inside the egg can be heard. From now on the nest should be examined daily, or at least every other day, so that any chicks that have died can be removed. The older the young are the more important this becomes. On the other hand, it is not necessary—at least not in

**Budgerigars will breed better in a less crowded breeding environment. If you opt for colony breeding, it is important that the birds be allowed to pair off on own their accord.**

With the variety of colors found in budgerigar genetics, breeders look forward to the results each particular mating will bring.

*Crop: a pouchlike enlargement in a bird's gullet in which food is stored.*

the early stages—to take the unfertilized eggs away. They give warmth and support to the very small chicks. For this reason, there is not the slightest need for the aviculturist who breeds for propagation to check whether the eggs have been fertilized. Impatience would do more harm than good. The breeder must on no account lose patience and do anything to speed up the process of hatching. Where the birds are being kept correctly, healthy chicks hatch unaided. In fact, the ability to hatch is an important indicator that the chick is fit to live.

### FEEDING OF THE YOUNG

In the early stages the feeding of the young is generally taken on by the hen alone, i.e., after the cock has filled her crop with food. Later the female goes to the dish and gets the food herself and the male takes part in the direct feeding of the young. The begging noises made by the young have a stimulating, or even a trigger, effect on the feeding drive of the parent birds. The newly-hatched chicks are fed lying on their backs. The female feeds them a yellowish-looking pap during the first few days. Then, from

**An affectionate budgie pair. Budgies are quite demonstrative in expressing their happiness with a mate.**

Its small size make a budgie easy to care for and easy to accommodate even in the smallest of apartments.

*Green food: any of a variety of green-colored vegetation that can be fed to birds. Includes grasses, such as chickweed, and cultivated vegetables, such as spinach.*

the third or fourth day, the crop-contents fed to the young is more solid. Particles of green food were found inside the crops of two-day-old chicks, however, and occasionally even a grain of millet. In the past it was thought that, similar to pigeons, young budgerigars were fed on "crop milk." In 1933 it was established that the liquid pap which was found inside the crop of both parent animals during the incubation period and fed to the young budgerigars in the first few days of life was identical to the food substance originating from the proventriculus. Later it was shown that the mucous membrane inside the crop of feeding hens does not have any glands.

For the budgerigar parents the feeding period is a very strenuous time. It was observed that the young of a pair the keeper allowed to breed in his study were being fed at intervals of half an hour to an hour throughout the day. How keen the adult animals are varies. Another aviculturist talks about hens which only allow themselves to be fed at the entrance-hole of the box, "and if their husband is too slow for their liking, they come outside and beat him up. If he still fails to fill them up again at the desired speed, they fill their crops themselves but then take longer to pre-digest the food."

**Opposite: Two newly born chicks and an unhatched egg are cared for by the hen. Baby birds require no care on your part. Just be sure to provide a proper diet for the hen.**

**Although budgies of today live happily in captivity, they still exhibit many behavioral traits established by their wild ancestors.**

*Nestling: a young bird that is not yet ready to leave the parental nest.*

### THE PHYSICAL DEVELOPMENT OF THE YOUNG

At first the young are pinkish-red, almost naked, and blind. At the age of seven to eight days they are covered in fluffy down. They open their eyes at the age of eight to ten days. The feathers begin to grow at about two weeks. While the quills are growing and have not yet burst through the young birds look positively "bristly." Soon the colors can be discerned.

The weight of the young depends on the genetic make-up of the parent animals. One breeder established average weights in normal budgerigars. He found that a chick which had just hatched and weighed 1 g (.035 ounce) increased its weight by 200% within the first two days. Thereafter the daily weight gain remained fairly stable at 23 g (.8 ounce) up to the 18th day when it dropped to a mere 1 g (.035 ounce) until the 23rd day. He noted that from the 24th day onward the nestlings moved about a lot inside the box; he could hear the tripping and the flapping of their wings. At this time the nestlings suffered a very slight weight loss (which has also been observed with regard to other species of parrots during the pre-fledging period) until they fledged, weighing 37 g (1.25 ounces).

**One of the greatest pleasures of budgerigar keeping is the opportunity to breed them and, hopefully, to produce a new color variety.**

The difference in weight between the young from one particular brood is considerable. For example, looking at a brood of four young which hatched one after the other, then the oldest chick weighs eleven times as much as the youngest which just hatched. The variations are even more pronounced where broods of eight young are concerned. Then the oldest already weighs 32 g (1.12 ounces)—less in practice—by the time the youngest has hatched weighing 1 g (.035 ounce). At first the chicks lie on top of each other, the smallest at the bottom as a rule. They are warmed by the mother. Provided the young are in good health and there are no major disturbances, they form a large heap like this even when they lie uncovered because the mother has had to leave the box.

What is the maximum number of young the parent animals are able to rear? It has been emphasized that it would be wrong to give any hard

*"The difference in weight between the young from one particular brood is considerable."*

**Budgerigars can be quite vocal, especially during courtship.**

**A mauve budgerigar. Some budgie fanciers prefer a heavy, stocky bird such as this.**

Head study of a light green budgerigar. While breeding for color may be the most important reason for your pursuit of the budgie hobby, your first concern should be the production of healthy, hardy birds.

A budgerigar that is routinely kept inside may enjoy the opportunity to be outdoors in sunshine and fresh air. Be sure to put the cage in a safe location and check it periodically.

and fast rules in this respect since every breeding pair is different: for some pairs three young are too much—this applies to show budgerigars—while others are able to rear five to six young without any difficulty. One can expect normal, healthy budgerigars to raise four to six young quite easily. Anything above that would cause problems, however. Where there are eight young, or even more, a second brood should not be permitted.

Younger well-fed nestlings have a large crop which visibly protrudes and a fat little tummy. This makes them rather clumsy. They cannot fledge until these two prominences have receded somewhat. Another prerequisite, of course, is that the plumage is complete (even if it has not yet grown to its full length). All this is the case at the age of about 30 days.

**FLEDGING**

Here, too, there are variations and they depend on the nutritional state and on heredity. Furthermore, young birds which grow up inside a low, broad box venture to the entrance-hole a bit earlier than those which grow up inside an upright box and have to climb up first. In the aviary where the box hangs high up the young pluck up the courage to leave the box at a rather later stage than do those in the cage where the jump to the ground is not very far. The fledged young continue to be fed for a while, usually by the male. They quickly learn to feed themselves, particularly if they are offered the favorite spray millet,which always gives them something to play

A yellow-face graywing budgerigar.

with and occupy themselves with at the same time. Before the last young of the brood has fledged the hen generally already starts to produce the new clutch.

At first the fledged young still move clumsily. The ability to fly may be innate, but aiming and landing have to be learned. They are frequently found sitting on the ground. Before separating them from the parents the aviculturist must be absolutely sure that they are able to feed themselves quite independently.

**An opaline gray-green budgerigar.**

*"The ability to fly may be innate, but aiming and landing have to be learned."*

**A cinnamon gray-green budgerigar.**

### CLEANLINESS OF THE NURSERY

One breeder states that some of the hens in his possession had actually taken the feces of the young outside the box, but these had been exceptional cases. Often the aviculturist only needs to clean or change the box after a brood has been reared. The "wet feeders," on the other hand, cause the breeder a lot of work. Here he occasionally has to change the box several times during the course of a brood. Sometimes he

*Fostering: the process whereby a breeding pair is used to raise young other than their own. This practice is utilized to save chicks that otherwise would die without the care of their parents.*

even needs to wash the feet of the young or the young themselves. It is of advantage if all the nest-boxes one owns are identical. Then a dirty one can readily be exchanged for a pre-warmed clean one. If the new box differs from the old one even only very slightly, it is sometimes not accepted.

### THE EXCHANGING OF CHICKS AND EGGS

Strange eggs or chicks, on the other hand, are less likely to be rejected by the budgerigars. Fostering may become necessary when one breeding partner falls ill or dies. (Aviculturists who breed show budgerigars also use this method systematically.) Young birds which are already a bit larger can also be reared by the male alone, provided there are not too many of them.

In their own box, budgerigars even feed young cockatiels—only as much and for as long as they would be able to feed their own young, however, which of course is not sufficient for cockatiels. A breeder once tried to use budgerigars as foster parents for lovebirds (*Agapornis personata*). One of the lovebirds hatched and was fed along with the budgerigar pair's own two chicks, although the redder the lovebird's beak became the less food it received. The feeding drive is stronger, of course, when the begging behavior of the young is healthy and appropriate for the species.

**Playgrounds designed for budgies will keep them entertained and amused. The varying thicknesses of such units are excellent for exercising your pet's toes.**

A budgie's perch should always be clean: free of droppings and food matter. Your pet shop offers handy utensils that aid in the cleaning of perches.

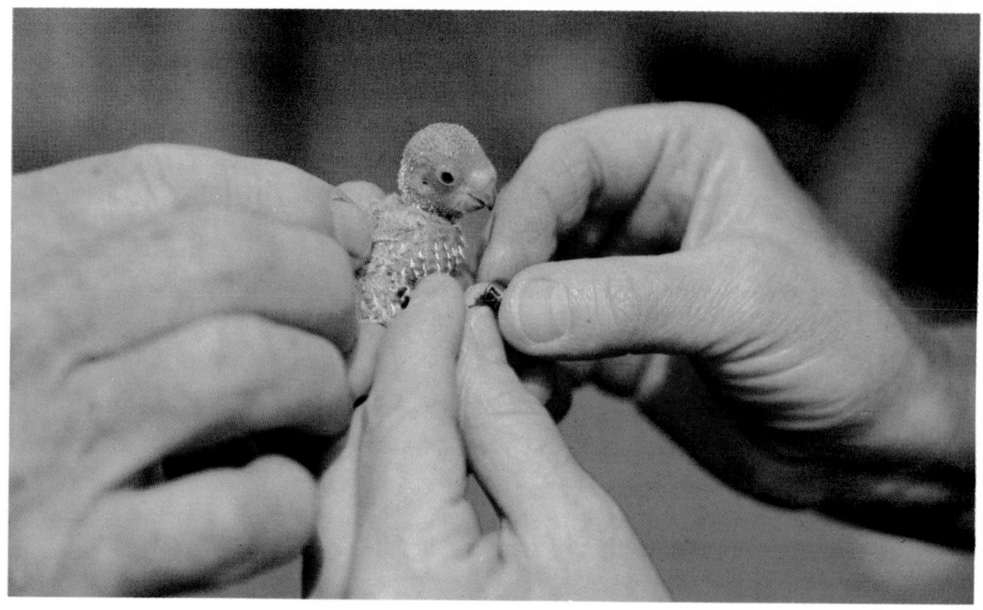

**Ringing is an invaluable aid for the budgie breeder. It can assist him with his record keeping of the color varieties that he produces.**

## RINGING

There are no hard and fast rules with regard to the timing. In extreme cases the closed ring can be put on on the fifth day. In the least favorable case the ring only stays in position if slipped on as late as on the eleventh day. The procedure is as follows: The ring is gently pulled over the three longest toes and the fourth, smallest, toe is then put through with the aid of a thin stick (such as a toothpick). The novice who has not had

**The identifying ring or band should be seamless and should have the correct identification number on it. Be sure all the chick's toes can move freely after you have completed the ringing procedure.**

Color breeders must take care not to overly inbreed their birds. Inbreeding will strengthen good points in the young, but it will also strengthen the bad points.

Attractive in appearance and delightful in behavior, the budgerigar can make a fine pet for people of all ages.

Budgies are avid chewers, so choose a metal cage as opposed to a wooden one.

If you want to train your budgie to talk, it might not be a good idea to provide him with a mirror. The feathered companion he sees in the mirror will divert his attention from you.

any practice is advised to make the first attempt at a rather early stage. If the ring slips off and lies inside the box the next day, the procedure has to be repeated. It is important never to use force when putting on the ring. Open rings are put on after fledging, at the very latest before the birds are sold or given away.

*Netting: the procedure of capturing and securing a free-flying bird by means of a net.*

### CATCHING AND REMOVING BIRDS

In certain circumstances it may be possible to remove young birds with one's bare hands. Netting causes the least agitation among the birds since this is the quickest way to catch them. That there must never be more than one bird in the net goes without saying. A bite from a budgerigar can be very painful. To prevent biting, immobilize the bird's head by holding it between the thumb and index finger. Where young birds are concerned this precaution is often unnecessary since they do not (yet) bite in any case.

### THE SHOW BREEDER

A highly respected aviculturist advises show breeders to accommodate young budgerigars in transitional cages after separating them from the parents. These cages should have adequate flying-space and be placed at eye-level. He then attaches show cages (special cages intended for exhibiting) to them from time to time and lures the young birds inside them, with spray millet, for short periods so that they get used to them. His further advice to the show breeders is to talk to such young birds a lot and to "train" them, i.e., to carefully get them to move from one perch to another. The calm behavior expected of them in front of the judge at a show is easiest to instill when the birds are still quite young. Success in this respect is important especially for the animal's own sake, since a bird which has not been acclimatized properly and therefore panics and anxiously dashes about is obviously not happy.

*"The calm behavior expected of them [budgerigars] at a show is easiest to instill when the birds are still quite young."*

**A pair of budgies: lutino and normal violet. A lovely flowering branch can be a nice accent for a budgie cage provided it is nonpoisonous and chemically untreated.**

Hand taming a budgie requires patience and persistence on your part. Even if your pet has already learned to accept your nearby presence, approach him slowly and calmly.

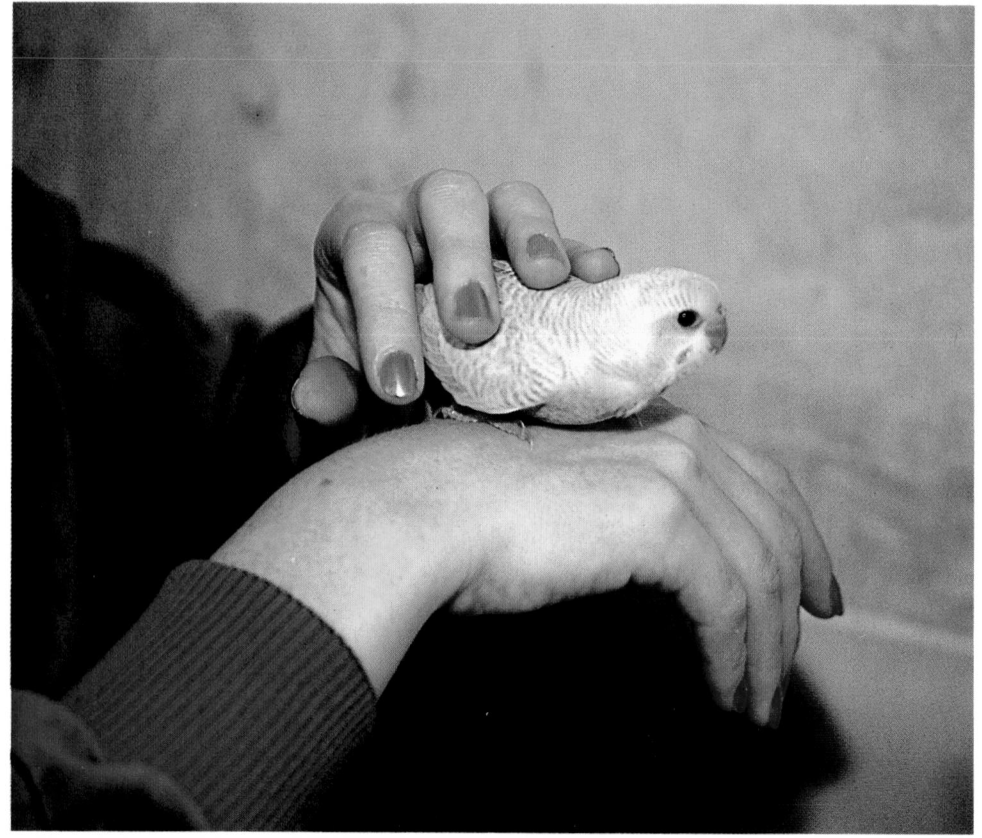

It is very rewarding to have a pet budgie stay calm and relaxed while he perches on your hand. Some fanciers like to softly talk or whistle to their budgie during a training session.

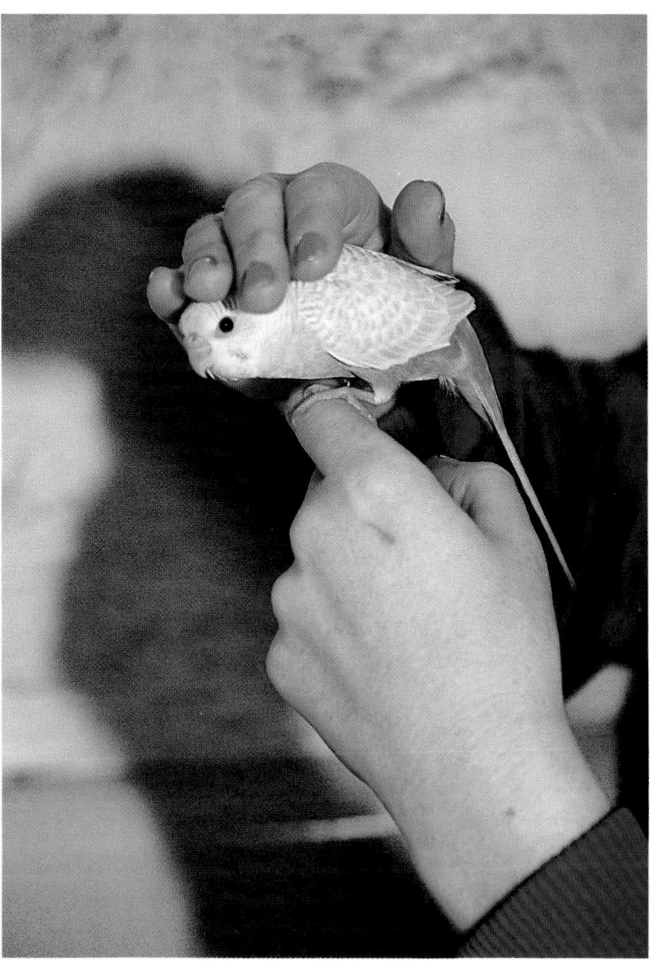

**Many pet budgies enjoy having their heads gently stroked. If your budgie doesn't enjoy such a practice, he may let you know it with a (harmless) little peck.**

**When training your budgie, there should be no distractions. A calm, quiet environment will help to keep his attention focused on you.**

# Dangers and Possible Mistakes

**Unless indisposed or too old, a budgie displays an alert, intelligent look that makes him an appealing pet.**

### NEGATIVE CONSEQUENCES OF FORCED PAIRINGS

When the aviculturist finds that a clutch is not being incubated, that the eggs are being devoured, that the hatched young are not being fed, that they are being plucked, injured, or even pecked to death, the reason for this may be that force was used in the pairing-up. If two birds which have not yet come together, or where the female has an aversion to the partner, are given stimulating food such as germinated wheat, then the breeding drive is often triggered but the breeding behavior may be disturbed.

*Forced pairing: selection, by a breeder, of a particular male bird and a particular female bird for the purpose of breeding them. This practice is the opposite of allowing a bird to select a mate of its choice.*

**Budgerigars come in many color varieties and patterns, all of which have been produced by breeders in small home aviaries.**

*"If a bird which had already found a partner in the aviary is abruptly separated from it and put into a compartment with a different bird, the inevitable outcome is extreme agitation. . . ."*

Unpleasant experiences can also result when one removes the birds from a community aviary and puts them into separate boxes in pairs in accordance with one's own ideas, without taking the birds' wishes into account. If a bird which had already found a partner in the aviary is abruptly separated from it and put into a compartment with a different bird, the inevitable outcome is extreme agitation, perhaps even a serious fight. It is not enough to make sure that two birds which have been forcibly separated cannot see one another. While they are able to hear each other, their agitated screaming can not only prevent them from mating with the new partner but can also irritate such pairs as are already in harmony. If the breeder wants to dissolve an existing bond (sometimes he has no alternative—for example, when two siblings are determined to mate with

**This photo dramatizes the length of a budgerigar's wings when fully extended, which makes it such a swift flyer.**

If your budgie has been housed alone for a long time, he may not accept a new bird. Keep this in mind if you plan to have a budgie family eventually.

**Budgerigars are hardy birds and, given proper care, can thrive in captivity.**

*"Birds with deformities or abnormalities of the plumage . . . must on no account be allowed to reproduce themselves."*

**Preening is an enjoyable activity for budgies as well as for many other types of birds.**

each other), he must separate the partners several weeks before the breeding cycle begins.

**BIRDS WHICH ARE UNSUITABLE FOR BREEDING**

It is obvious that only healthy birds should be selected for breeding. Birds with deformities or abnormalities of the plumage (above all the so-called "runners" which are incapable of flying) must on no account be allowed to reproduce themselves. Breeding pairs that have already produced "runners" or young with deformities or perhaps broods with a very high nestling mortality should at least be separated and each paired up with another

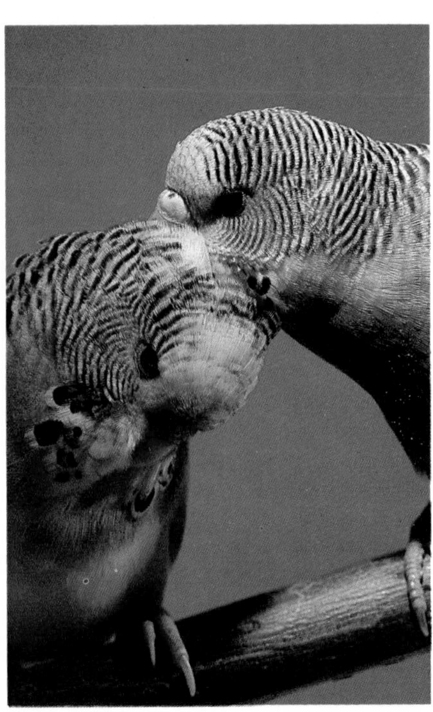

partner so that it can be established which animal is transmitting the negative phenomena. Birds that have already devoured eggs, plucked young or killed them are also best excluded from further breeding, likewise their surviving young.

Where budgerigar hens do not feed the chicks of their first brood, it is also possible that these hens are still too young. In that case they are simply not mature enough for breeding. I once observed such a process of maturation in a cockatiel hen. It had derived from the first brood of the year. During the fourth brood (which I do not normally permit) it allowed itself to be mounted by the foster father (not a blood-relation) and laid eggs at the same time as its foster mother. At first it took only a sporadic part in the

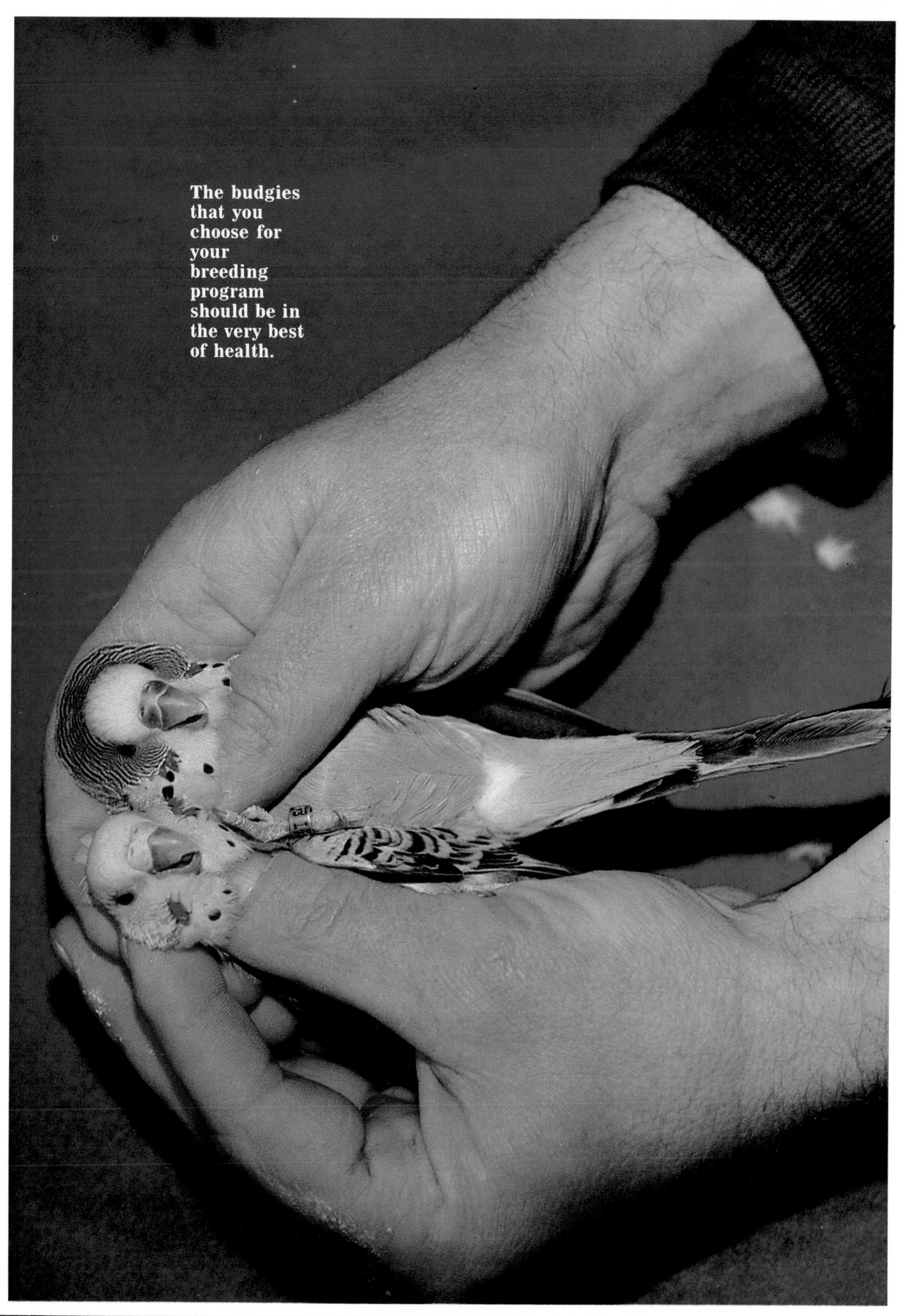

The budgies that you choose for your breeding program should be in the very best of health.

*"Breeding with older budgerigars can pose a problem, particularly if these birds have been kept in isolation."*

incubating and the subsequent feeding and warming of the young, but as time went by its contribution to the rearing of the young intensified. By the time the young had fledged the young female had become solely responsible for feeding them.

Breeding with older budgerigars can pose a problem, particularly if these birds have been kept in isolation. While they are within the age range for breeding they should still be capable of raising a few broods. I have a cockatiel hen, kept on her own and completely tame for three years, which first laid eggs at the age of four years and from the age of five onwards reared young very reliably at regular intervals. If the budgerigar can cause us greater difficulties in this respect, it is undoubtedly due to the fact that its

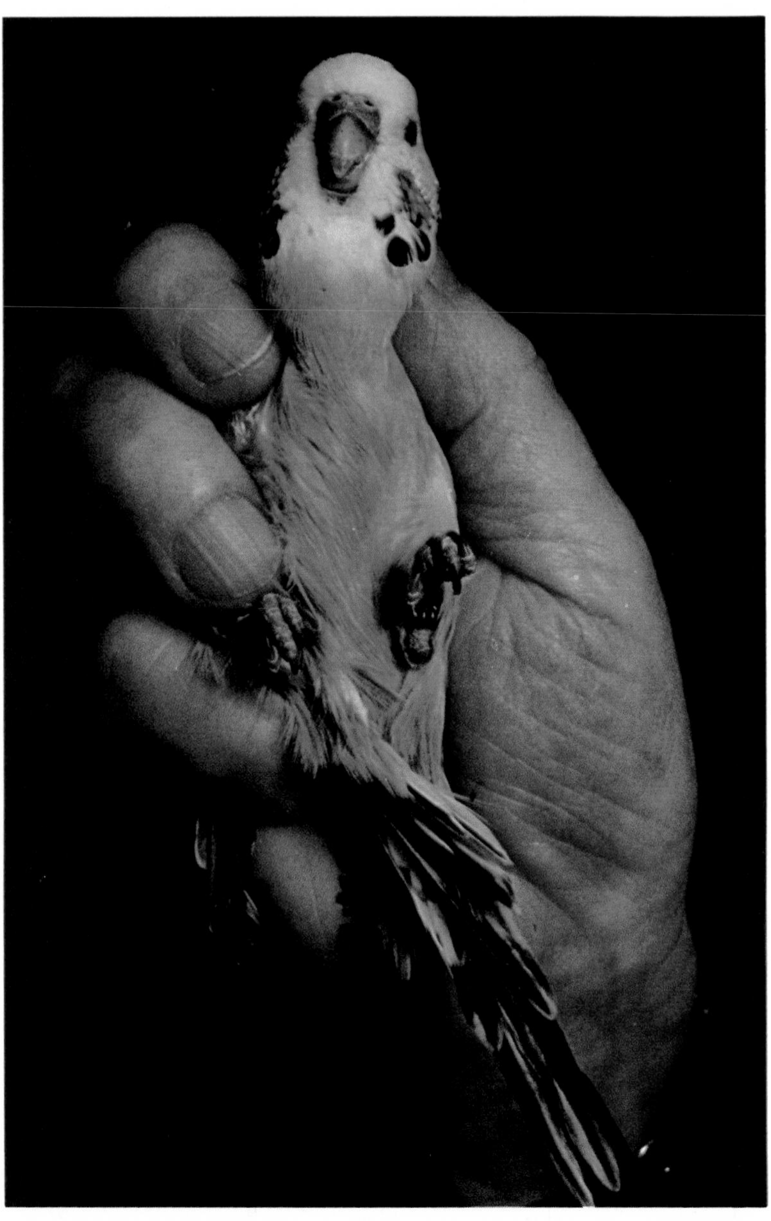

**As hardy as your budgie may be, he still should be checked regularly for any abnormalities or signs of illness.**

Always remember to plan all matings carefully, as preparedness can help to reduce the incidence of defective offspring.

**A natural vivacity underlies a budgie's interest in toys and therefore its trainability.**

*"One fundamental rule is that the breeder must not in any way disrupt the hen's breeding rhythm."*

domestication (and degeneration) is at a more advanced stage.

### DANGERS CAUSED BY THE BREEDER'S INTERVENTION

As we have seen earlier, a budgerigar hen generally accepts strange eggs and chicks that have been put into her nest, i.e., she tolerates minor changes to the nest. But she will not be forced to accept a changed nest-box. Basically, one can say: When the hen takes possession of a nest-box she removes all "foreign bodies," even eggs she herself has laid elsewhere. Once she has taken possession of the box, however, she accepts even strange eggs and young that lie inside it as her property, provided the aviculturist takes the hen's breeding rhythm into consideration.

One fundamental rule is that the breeder must not in any way disrupt the hen's breeding rhythm. For example, he should *not* take the unfertilized eggs away from her half-way through the breeding cycle in the hope that she will produce the much longed for young as quickly as possible. Either allow her to sit on those eggs for 18 days or put fertilized eggs of the same age from another pair underneath her. Do not remove the nest-box, towards the end of the breeding period, while the hen is still laying because a forced interruption of egg-laying can cause diseases of the female reproductive organs (egg binding, etc.). It is better to wait until the hen has completed the clutch. During the breeding cycle in the colony system on no account add new animals or pairs or provide a replacement for a partner that has become ill or has died.

**Budgies can be a source of enjoyment for people of all ages.**

*Egg binding: a condition that can occur in a female bird whereby it is unable to pass an egg through the cloacal passage.*

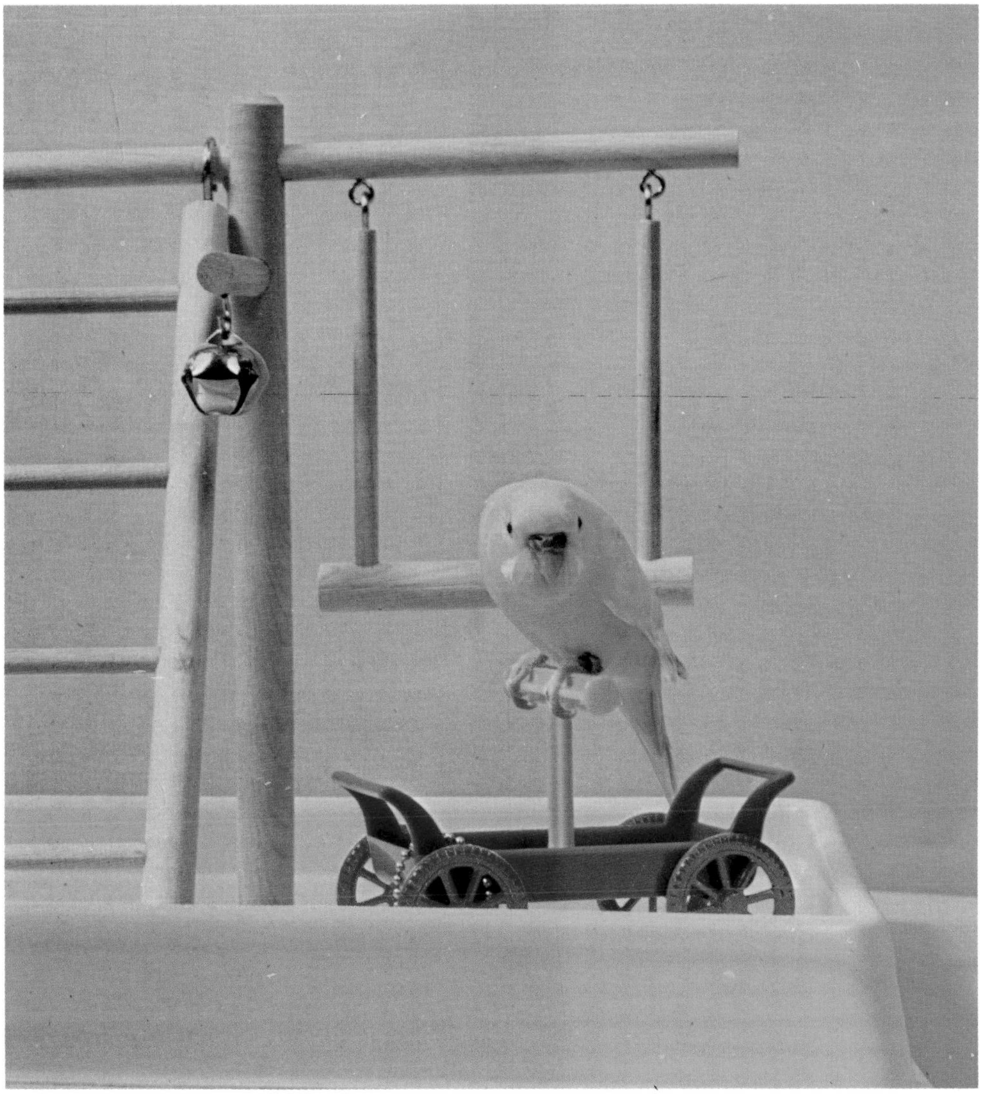

**An array of various budgie toys. All of these articles can be easily cleaned with soap and water.**

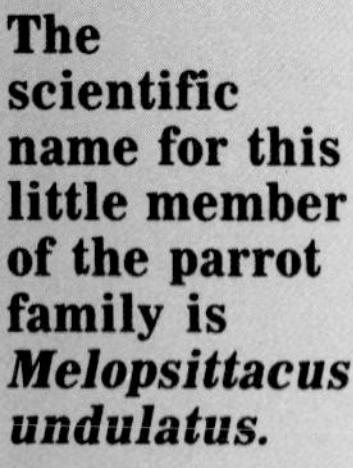

**The scientific name for this little member of the parrot family is *Melopsittacus undulatus.***

A striking palette of color and interesting pattern mutations have contributed to the popularity of the budgerigar.

**If you let your budgie out of his cage for regular exercise periods, be sure that he does not have access to such things as poisonous plants.**

*Aspergillosis: an infectious disease caused by certain fungi of the genus* Aspergillus.

**Preening may occupy a considerable amount of your budgie's time.**

**CONTROL**

During hot weather the heat can build up inside the box. Where this danger exists the breeder should open the lid of the box; sometimes a crack is sufficient. It is necessary, also, to check how soiled the box has become and to have a look at the litter. Where mold has formed, the breeder must replace and disinfect the box. A case has been described where the litter consisted of peat and the latter contained fungus spores which caused an outbreak of aspergillosis.

**CHANGES AMONG THE STOCK**

The owner of a stud not only sells animals but also buys new ones, exchanges birds, takes them to exhibitions where they come into contact with other birds, takes supernumerary birds to some bird-market or other and, if they have remained unsold, brings them home again. In short, there is a constant danger for the birds to contract infectious diseases. A single bird excreting worms' eggs in its feces can cause the entire stock to become infested with worms. One bird excreting *Salmonella* bacteria in its droppings (the bird itself appearing clinically healthy) can cause all the birds in the stud to fall ill within a few days and a large proportion of them to die.

Still widely feared even today is psittacosis. This disease has brought a decisive influence to bear on the history of parrot—and hence—budgerigar keeping. Until the early 1930s there were repeated epidemic-like outbreaks of the disease, notably

**The budgie owner who spends considerable time caring for and observing his bird will know what a healthy bird looks like and will quickly notice when something is amiss.**

*Psittacosis: a virus-caused disease that can afflict parrots and other birds and is communicable to humans.*

*Ornithosis: The viral disease psittacosis as it occurs in non-psittacine birds.*

among people who came into contact with parrots imported from overseas. In some cases the disease—serious infectious broncho-pneumonia—ran a fatal course. Hence, "psittacosis regulations" were drawn up and implemented. In spite of these measures, however, the psittacosis was not eradicated. (This disease affects not only parrots. When occurring in other species of birds it is called ornithosis.) When it became possible to treat the infectious disease successfully with antibiotics, a relaxation of the regulations resulted.

In infected studs the young birds contract the disease in the nest. Other diseases can also be

**The use of wooden perches will help to keep your budgie's claws trim.**

Regularly cleaning and disinfecting your budgie's cage can help to combat harmful bacterial growth.

**Providing your budgie with a proper diet and keeping his surroundings and equipment clean are important factors in the bird's good health.**

*"... thorough and regular cleaning and disinfecting [of an aviary or cage] is strongly recommended."*

transmitted to the nestlings by the feeding adult birds, sometimes without the parent animals themselves showing any signs of disease.

**HYGIENE**

The progressive decline in the breeding performance in long established budgerigar studs, especially in those with a high population density, is not a nutritional problem or the consequence of degenerative phenomena which are genetic in origin but is first and foremost a problem of hygiene. Veterinarians suggest a reduction in the population density, and thorough and regular cleaning and disinfecting is strongly recommended. Basically, disinfecting is effective only where it has been preceded by thorough cleaning. Where the floor consists of natural soil, the top 25 cm (10 inches) need to be removed and replaced. Merely digging is not sufficient since disease-producing organisms survive at a depth of up to 25 cm (10 inches). Natural soil, sand, or gravel can also be disinfected by means of a steam jet. Aviaries with concrete floors and breeding cages are, of course, much easier to disinfect.

Once or twice a year (in the fall and spring) everything should be

Captive-bred budgerigars are usually larger and heavier than bred-in-the-wild budgerigars.

*Red bird-mite: a small blood-sucking parasite that attacks many different bird types.*

thoroughly cleaned and disinfected. Between times the perches and the food and water bowls should be disinfected every so often. Nest-boxes must be thoroughly cleaned and disinfected before each use. All the perches should be scraped clean with a spatula before disinfecting them, the wire netting scrubbed with a wire-brush. Disinfectants are available in liquid form and as sprays. Food leftovers and droppings must be removed at regular intervals.

The aviculturist may have problems with mites (notably the "red bird-mite"). They can endanger the small nestlings in particular; they can generally be controlled easily and effectively with insecticides (sprays, liquid).

**If you own more than one budgerigar, cleaning the birds' living area will have to be done more frequently because of the greater accumulation of dirt.**

A natural branch can make a good perch due to the variations in width one piece of wood may contain. However, you must be sure that the wood has not been treated with chemicals of any kind.

**Its small size, cleanliness, and hardiness make the budgie an ideal pet.**

***Opposite:* A yellow-face blue budgie and a pied yellow budgie.**

*"... the breeder has to observe his birds for signs of disease at all times."*

**A gray-green budgerigar.**

## EXAMINATION OF FECES, DISPATCH OF DEAD BIRDS FOR AUTOPSY

Hygiene alone does not always keep the stock healthy, even in conjunction with the quarantine-like measures described earlier. A latent carrier of disease, a bird which excretes disease-producing organisms on an irregular basis can be a constant danger to the stock. It is always advisable to send samples of feces to a veterinary research laboratory for analysis from time to time. The fecal specimens must be fresh. If the result is negative, i.e., no bacteria or parasites have been found, this does not mean the bird is not a potential source of infection. This also applies where psittacosis is concerned. In other words, the breeder has to observe his birds for signs of disease at all times.

What goes for the result of a fecal examination also applies here. The possibility of an infectious disease can never quite be ruled out even if no bacteria or parasites have been found. Thus there was one occasion when the causal agent of pseudotuberculosis (not transmitted to man) could only be detected in my stock after I had sent the third brown-headed parrot chick to the research laboratory. Now I was able to treat the adult birds. Only after that had been done did the broods of the brown-headed parrots survive. If there are grounds to suspect that an animal has died of psittacosis, it is absolutely *essential* for the breeder to send it off for an autopsy. It goes without saying that this kind of examination serves a rather more important purpose than merely to satisfy one's curiosity.

**Budgerigars are the best known species of parrot. This bird is a dominant pied light green.**

*Salmonellosis: a disease caused by* Salmonella *bacteria.*

Readers who have now become worried about salmonellosis and psittacosis, the two diseases that can be contracted by human beings, should note the words of a veterinarian of experience: "The knowledge that diseases of birds can be transmitted to man must not, however, be allowed to lead to irrational fear and to detract from the pleasure in the hobby. Risks to human health exist everywhere."

**It is better to avoid sickness by learning how a budgie should be kept than trying to cure him after he has taken ill.**

**Given the proper attention and care, your budgie can be a happy, healthy pet.**

# Budgerigar Breeding: Pet Bird or Show Bird?

*Standard: a written description of what, ideally, a particular animal should look like.*

As distinct from mere propagation, "breeding" in this context refers to the deliberate, programmed mating of animals with a breeding goal in view. Where the budgerigar is concerned this goal is the ideal budgerigar in accordance with the Budgerigar Society's standard. The aviculturist strives to get as close as possible to the ideal budgerigar by means of constant selection, planned, guided matings, and crossing. Experienced breeders of show budgerigars always stress that "inbreeding" or "linebreeding" are unavoidable. "Inbreeding" denotes the mating of siblings, father × daughter, and mother × son. "Linebreeding" also describes matings between relatives, but here they are less closely related.

Many aviculturists proceed according to the simplest method: They obtain good birds from a breeding line at a reliable establishment and linebreed them.

Obviously only the best young animals are mated with the parent of the opposite sex. As a result of using this method it often produces very beautiful young birds which perhaps stand a chance of doing well at exhibitions. But in the long term, unfortunately, there is a high price to pay for this. Often one comes across budgerigar hens which are incapable of laying eggs. This is a blow, particularly for the novice breeder, who has only limited space and therefore can buy only a few birds. If he is unlucky, none of his pairs manage to raise healthy young. The responsible breeder of show budgerigars should, as a matter of principle, carry out test matings with birds derived by inbreeding to establish whether fertility and health have been preserved.

The following method for building up a show budgerigar strain is recommended: from one line, select a male bird and two female birds, not too closely related, to form the starting material.

*Fertility: the capacity to reproduce.*

**For breeding purposes, it is best to acquire two to three pairs, since budgies breed better when they can observe other pairs of their kind.**

**Always select the strongest, healthiest looking budgerigar that you can find.**

*Hen: a female bird.*

**Some breeders specialize in colors; some in only one or two colors; some in size, type, or new shades.**

Breed the male to both females. The next year breed the original male with the best young hen of the previous breedings. Also cross the best male from each original female with the original female that is not his mother.

In addition, very good young birds from the mating of the first year (but not full siblings) may be mated together.

Third year: Crossing with unrelated birds. For this, it is best to buy cocks, and they should show features which can be expected to improve the quality of one's own line. The novice is warned it would be a

Pet bird or show bird, you will love your budgie for his pleasing ways and lovely appearance.

*Show quality: an animal's possession of features and characteristics that can be judged as exemplifying, or approaching, the ideal appearance for an animal of its type.*

mistake, however, to wait impatiently and believe that all the flaws that are present can be ironed out instantly. From now on the breeder needs a great deal of intuition. He has to keep "crossing in" strange blood. Above all, the breeder needs patience and a sound knowledge of breeding and clearly not an impatient experimentation with inbreeding.

**THE SHOW RACE**

Budgerigar breeders who want to change from breeding pet quality budgerigars to show budgerigars must be prepared for setbacks in the early stages. A clear warning: budgerigars of the show quality do not as a rule breed as prolifically as the smaller, common or garden varieties. . . . This tends to apply to all animal races bred

**In many cases, budgies have been reared in roomy breeding cages or aviaries which afforded them a lot of space for movement. If you plan a show career for your budgie, he will have to become accustomed to a show cage.**

A healthy budgie is bright-eyed, alert, and inquisitive. If he is kept with other birds, he should be interested in socializing with them.

**As far as the shape and size of budgerigars is concerned, the science of genetics still has much to reveal.**

*"[With show birds] there are more unfertilized eggs and dead chicks inside the egg or at the nestling stage."*

specifically for performance or beauty. There are more unfertilized eggs and dead chicks inside the egg or at the nestling stage. One veterinarian notes regretfully, "A reduced fertility really only occurs in the show race. For decades and the world over, fertility was neglected as an element for selection in the breeding of show budgerigars. Type and color were given priority over fertility." Breeders might want to consider the following principle, formulated by one aviculturist who specializes in breeding show budgerigars: "The preservation of fertility and health must be given absolute priority in all cases." Making sure that this principle is applied in practice is one of the responsibilities of the Budgerigar Society and the local societies affiliated to it.

"These heavy show birds will never become widely

A yellow-winged light green budgerigar. Your pet shop stocks budgies in a variety of colors and patterns.

*"The owner of a tame budgerigar is not generally very interested in the length of the wings or the bird's deportment on the perch."*

available," says another renowned aviculturist, "but, then, that is not the idea." It is certainly true that these quiet birds are less suitable as household pets and could never hope to compete with the lively, high-spirited ordinary budgerigar in that respect. stout 'John Bulls' as the birds of the future."

**PROPAGATIVE BREEDING**

Thus, breeding budgerigars purely to multiply their numbers

**These six youngsters are from a single nest. The possibility of getting numerous colors from a single breeding pair accounts for a great deal of the interest in breeding for color.**

As for the ideal with regard to beauty: When the British show race became known in the early 1950s, by no means did all the breeders feel inclined to accept these birds as "the ideally beautiful." The above mentioned aviculturist states that he had not been particularly taken with them either: "We were used to lively, slender parakeets with bright colors and suddenly found ourselves confronted with these

continues to make sense. This type of breeding produces the pet budgerigar so popular in the home. The owner of a tame budgerigar is not generally very interested in the length of the wings or the bird's deportment on the perch. Nor is he concerned about purity of color—what matters to him is that the bird's color appeals to his personal sense of beauty. Sometimes, unfortunately, animals

***Opposite:*** **Light gray opaline budgerigar.**

*"Only a robust, healthy bird is suitable as a household pet."*

that are too small are offered for sale by backyard breeders and the customers are unaware of this. Their ignorance is exploited by "black sheep" among the breeders—they permit four broods or even more, which naturally has an adverse effect on the health both of the parent animals and the young birds. Uninformed people are easy to fool. Once at a bird show I saw an adult point at my white cockatiel (at that time still tame, kept on its own), which was standing beside my sulphur-crested cockatoo, and heard him say to his child, "Look, that's the young of the big bird." No wonder, then, that progressively smaller budgerigars can be sold as "nestlings" of an increasingly tender age!

**THE RESPONSIBILITY OF THE BREEDER**

In the last analysis, any budgerigar breeder who propagates budgerigars and sells young birds in an irresponsible manner is his own worst enemy. The bird fancier who wants to share his home with a tame pet has no intention—if he is a genuine bird-lover—to get "something new" every year. Only a robust, healthy bird is suitable as a household pet. Hens which are unsuitable for breeding may not necessarily be able to adapt to life in the home. It is a well-known fact that many tame females have a tendency to lay eggs. If such a female then dies a slow, miserable death—and is perhaps not the first bird the keeper has

**A playground affords a means of keeping a budgie happily occupied.**

Give your new budgie time to get accclimated to his new environment. This can take hours, and sometimes even days, because these birds differ individually just as much as people do.

**The white flight and tail feathers of a lutino budgerigar may need to be washed before the bird is entered in a show or sold to a customer.**

lost in this way—the owner eventually gets put off keeping budgerigars and may put other people off as well. The breeder's responsibility is a dual one: To the living creature and to the buyers who (at least in part) finance his hobby by taking the excess young birds from him.

*"The breeder's responsibility is a dual one: to the living creature and to the buyers. . . ."*

## COLOR VARIETIES OF THE BUDGERIGARS

The light-green budgerigar with the normal markings looks more or less the same as the wild bird in Australia. This coloring serves the purpose of camouflage. The budgerigars in Australia like to congregate on the shore of periodic watercourses in whose immediate proximity individual eucalyptus trees stand. In their tops the parakeets spend the best part of the day. And since they tend to sit about very sluggishly, barely moving and seldom calling, and because the green of their plumage is virtually identical to that of the eucalyptus leaves, they are excellently camouflaged there. Often one does not spot them until they fly off within a few meters from the approaching human. Hence they largely rely on their good camouflage color, sit tight for as long as possible when danger threatens and literally do not make their escape

Opaline cobalt male budgerigar.

*Genetics: the study of heredity and how its variations are manifested in living organisms.*

until the last moment.

In 1840 the first wild budgerigars from Australia were imported into Great Britain. In 1855 the first successful breeding attempt in captivity was reported in Germany. By 1955 (100 years later), about 300 different color varieties and shades were known, surely something which is unparalleled in the history of animal breeding. The breeders exploited the wild budgerigar's natural tendency towards mutations, and with the aid of an increasing knowledge of genetics,it became possible to fix the desired color shades. In their natural habitat, budgerigars which deviate in color from the natural camouflage color, notably the blue ones, cannot survive for long. Furthermore, mutations are generally inherited *recessively* (that is, they are suppressed in favor of an alternative character), which means without the breeder's intervention they soon disappear. We differentiate between the green series and the blue series, and all other colors are derived from these.

**Young budgies are sometimes called barheads because of the dark striping on the forehead. This is a gray-green barhead male.**

**The color of a budgerigar has nothing to do with the bird's value as a pet.**

Additional factors which influence the color and markings of the budgerigar's plumage are: dark factor (e.g. light-green or dark-green, etc.), markings, albinism (absence of pigment). The inheritance of green is *dominant* (showing its effect) over that of blue; so is that of gray. Gray-green is dominant over gray. An example: green × blue will produce nothing but green youngsters. The latter are not homozygous (i.e., they do not just carry the green factor), however, but heterozygous (split, carrying the color factors from both parents). They are, therefore, described as green split for blue, which is written green/blue. If such a green bird which is heterozygous for blue is mated with a

*"The inheritance of green is dominant over that of blue."*

homozygous blue bird, the progeny will also include birds with a blue plumage color. For the type of improvement necessary for show breeding, the aviculturist requires gray or gray-green birds, which the majority of fanciers consider less attractive. Some budgerigar breeders in Australia catch wild budgerigar cocks and cross their existing stock with them. What is interesting is that the young produced by these matings are more lively in color than those whose parents have both been raised in captivity. They are also particularly viable.

How the plumage colors in the budgerigar are produced is explained as follows: In the majority of cases, blue is what is known as a structural color which occurs when air-filled colorless alveolar cells with walls made opaque by canaliculi lie on a dark background. If the outer horny layer is yellow, the feather appears green—in other words, one can see the blue color through a layer of yellow. The color of the ordinary green budgerigar is an example of this. Where, as a result of selective breeding in captivity, the yellow outer layer is absent in the

*"Blue is what is known as a structural color which occurs when air-filled colorless alveolar cells with walls made opaque by canaliculi lie on a dark background."*

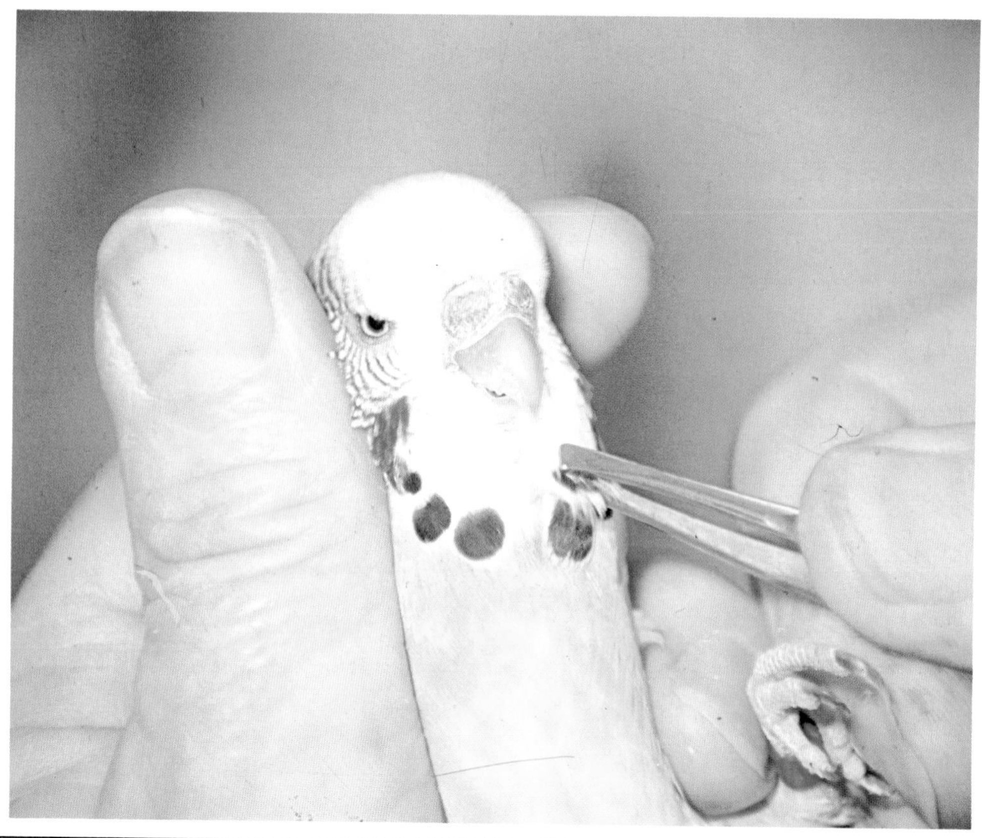

**Exhibition budgerigar hen having her mask trimmed with tweezers.**

**In their natural habitat, budgies that deviate in color from the natural camouflage color cannot survive for long.**

*"Budgerigar colors include: green, olive, blue, violet, gray, yellow, white, in various shades, color combinations, and plumage markings."*

budgerigar, the bird looks blue. Where the underlying brown layer necessary for the blue effect is not present,the bird appears yellow. In the white budgerigar both layers are absent. If a blue feather is completely saturated with water so that the air disappears from the alveolar cells, it looks blackish. Looking at its underside, against the light, produces the same effect. And a green parrot that has become absolutely drenched looks gray-brown.

Budgerigar colors include: green, olive, blue, violet, gray, yellow, white, in various shades, color combinations, and plumage markings.

**A budding breeder would do well to start small and purchase a few good birds instead of many of low quality.**

**Keeping budgerigars in good health will preserve the beautiful colors that careful breeding has created.**

# Suggested Reading

*T.F.H. Publications' bird books combine sensible, practical advice from world-renowned experts with beautiful and informative bird photographs.*

The following books by T.F.H. Publications are available at pet shops everywhere.

**THE COMPLETE BIRDS OF THE WORLD by Michael Walters (H-1022)**

This book lists every bird species in the world and gives for each the family relationship, range, common and scientific name and related important data. One of the finest ornithological works ever produced. Illustrated with full-color photos. Hard cover, 8½ x 11″, 704 pages.

**PARROTS OF THE WORLD by Joseph M. Forshaw (PS-753)**

For bird lovers of all types, this book covers every species and subspecies of parrot in the world, including those recently extinct. Information is presented on distribution, status, habitats, and general habits. Illustrated with full-color photos. Hard cover, 9½ x 12½″, 584 pages.

**BIRD DISEASES: AN INTRODUCTION TO THE STUDY OF BIRDS IN HEALTH AND DISEASE by Drs. L. Arnall and I.F. Keymer (H-964)**

Requires a basic familiarity with biology to be understood, but experienced bird lovers can recognize symptoms and diseases from the many illustrations. Illustrated with full-color photos. Hard cover, 6 x 9″, 528 pages.

**DISEASES OF CAGE BIRDS by Dr. Elisha Burr (H-1096)**

The definitive text dealing with the diseases of companion birds. Easy to read and easy to follow, this book is invaluable to everyone involved with the bird fancy. Illustrated with full-color photos. Hard cover, 8½ x 11″, 247 pages.

**ENCYCLOPEDIA OF BUDGERIGARS by Georg A. Radtke (H-1027)**
An authoritative and up-to-date book that covers completely the care and breeding of budgerigars. Also includes sections on disease prevention and treatment, training, and the origin and development of color varieties. Illustrated with full-color photos. Hard cover, 5½ x 8″, 320 pages.

**BUDGERIGAR HANDBOOK by Ernest H. Hart (H-901)**
Presents sensible, easy-to-follow recommendations about selecting and caring for budgerigars. Illustrated with full-color photos. Hard cover, 5½ x 8½″, 251 pages.

**THE JOY OF BUDGERIGARS by Howard Richmond (PS-799)**
An indispensable reference work for everyone interested in budgerigars. Illustrated with full-color photos. Hard cover, 5½ x 8″, 96 pages.

**BEGINNING WITH BUDGERIGARS by Anne Ray Streeter (PS-839)**
This book concentrates on discussing in detail the basics of selecting and caring for a budgerigar. Provides needed information about how to choose the best bird right through how to sex and breed budgies. Illustrated with full-color photos. Soft cover, 5½ x 8″, 128 pages.

**TAMING AND TRAINING BUDGERIGARS by Risa Teitler (KW-070)**
Contains informative and practical information about the taming and training of budgerigars. Illustrated with full-color photos. Hard cover, 5½ x 8″, 128 pages.

**BUDGERIGARS by Georg A. Radtke (KW-011)**
This book provides comprehensive information for the beginning budgie enthusiast as well as for the advanced hobbyist. Illustrated with full-color photos. Hard cover, 5½ x 8″, 128 pages.

**BREEDING BUDGERIGARS by Cessa Feyerabend and Dr. Matthew M. Vriends (PS-761)**
This book clearly and concisely introduces all of the steps in successfully breeding budgerigars. Illustrated with full-color photos. Soft cover, 5½ x 8″, 192 pages.

**ALL ABOUT BREEDING BUDGERIGARS by Mervin F. Roberts (PS-804)**
Novice budgerigar owners who want to start their own breeding programs and veteran budgerigar breeders who need information on how to improve what they've started will derive great benefit from this practical, useful book. Illustrated with full-color photos. Hard cover, 5½ x 8″, 96 pages.

*T.F.H. Publications publishes books about every popular bird and bird group.*

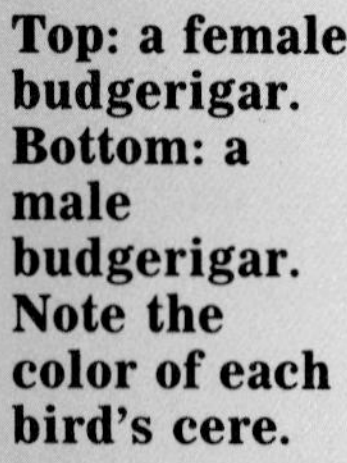

**Top: a female budgerigar. Bottom: a male budgerigar. Note the color of each bird's cere.**

# Index



*Use this Index to help you quickly locate a particular topic.*

**TS-138**
**Keeping**
**and**
**Breeding**
**Budgerigars**